Catholic Traditional & Black

in Anthology and Discourse

Catholic Traditional & Black

in Anthology and Discourse

David L. Gray, Editor

Saint Dominic's Media
Belleville, Illinois

© 2022 David L. Gray
All Rights Reserved

"Catholic, Traditional & Black: In Anthology and Discourse". Contributors: Monsignor C. Eugene Morris S.T.L. (Foreword), Arlena Brown (Contributor), Eric Phillips (Contributor), Géraldine Précil (Contributor), Jackson Pickney (Contributor), and Anita G. Gorman (Consulting Editor)

Published by Saint Dominic's Media, Inc., 120 W. Washington St., Suite 8225, Belleville, IL 62220. The Mission of Saint Dominic's Media is to acquire, develop, produce, market, and distribute works of non-fiction and fiction that reflect the Dominican spirit of a life devoted to liturgical prayer, study of sacred truth, and zeal for the salvation of souls, for an audience that is seeking a richer, deeper spiritual life while living in the world. We seek to do all things Deum verum, for the truth of God. www.saintdominicsmedia.com

Printed in the United States of America

19 29 21 22 23 24 25   8 7 6 5 4 3 2

BISAC Categories:
RELIGION / Christianity / Catholic
RELIGION / Christian Living / Inspirational
RELIGION / Christian Living / Personal Memoirs

ISBN-13: 979-8-9857040-2-0 (Hardcover)

Venerable Pierre Toussaint,
Pray for Us

Venerable Henriette DeLille,
Pray for Us

Venerable Father Augustus Tolton,
Pray for Us

Servant of God Mother Mary Lange,
Pray for Us

Servant of God Julia Greeley,
Pray for Us

contents

Introduction viii
Foreword, by Monsignor C. Eugene Morris, S.T.L. ix
God's Prodigal People - A Preface, by David L. Gray) 1
The Day Life Changed, by Arlena Brown 35
I Found My Identity In the Catholic Mass, by Eric Phillips ... 44
My First Black Catholic Priest, by Géraldine Précil 60
I Am My Ancestor's Wildest Dream, by Jackson Pickney ... 83
My Skin Color Wasn't Enough, by David L. Gray 95
Novena to Father Augustus Tolton 109

introduction

Here are stories of five people of God whose lives have been dramatically changed and enriched for having discovered the penetrating beauty of Catholic traditional liturgy and the permanence of traditional Catholic values and devotions, which have oiled the lamp through which they seek first the Kingdom of God and His righteousness. These five people also happen to be identified as Black Americans but have been inspired to live their lives through their Catholic faith, rather than through society's race constructs.

foreword
Monsignor C. Eugene Morris, S.T.L.

The polemics of the modern age make normal discourse difficult at the best of times, impossible at the worst of times. It is now commonplace to allow self-described and self-proclaimed identity to be the only truth in conversation. Consequently, human conversation and rational dialogue are impeded by the inability of a common language, shared identity, and objective, immutable truths. It appears that everyone has gone into their own corners from whence they only venture when they encounter those of like mind, identity, and common language. This would not be such a bad thing if the leftist agenda that has permeated society and culture allowed for differing views and opinions giving everyone the peace to exist in their own corner.

Those who trumpet freedom and license, those who have turned traditional morality on its head, those who have pulled God from His heaven and declared Him to be just another philosopher are not satisfied with staying in their own corner. Instead, not only have they appointed themselves the arbiters of all truth, but then also demanded they everyone fall in line and accept their version of "truth". The contradictions and hypocrisy would be laughable if real people were not losing their jobs, being removed from the public square, and being silenced for preaching and teaching the truth. With this as the backdrop, David L. Gray has brought

Monsignor C. Eugene Morris, S.T.L.

together voices from a community often neglected and rarely heard. They join his voice in reminding us that there is only one truth, the truth Himself – God almighty.

In his volume: *Catholic, Traditional and Black: in Anthology and Discourse*, Mr. Gray brings together Black voices who not only reject the dominant sociological narrative as to identity and cultural experience but who also defy the common perceptions of what Black religious experience is and ought to be. If the current cultural climate trumpets the lie of Black sociological uniformity, so too does the dominant understanding of the reality of Catholicism in the life of Black Americans. How timely to have a series of reflections that dispel these myths and provide an authentic voice to the truth of Catholicism to reach through history, culture, and polemics and provide the source of peace and salvation for the whole world.

It is difficult to be a Catholic in the world today and often difficult to be one in the Church Herself. It is also true that navigating the world as a Black American is at times an arduous task where the road map is not always clear as to which direction one should follow. To bring together the Catholic identity and wed it to the Black experience makes those who choose this path brave, crazy, or maybe both. What is valuable about these reflections is that answer to this delicate balancing act of who I am and what my place is in the world is arrived at through choosing the only course that matters: the one set forth by Christ Himself. The title of this book already provides us insights into the lens through which one sees the world – we are Catholics first and foremost. From there we make decisions about the other communities in which we live by immersing those other communities into our Catholic lives.

Sadly, given the sometimes confusing and chaotic reality of the modern Church, it is not always an easy decision to make or a clear immersion to undertake. The Church is struggling in the modern age and appears more comfortable adapting Herself to the age instead of evangelizing and transforming culture. Herein lies the value of tradition. Adhering to traditional forms of worship is not nostalgia or fear, but a solid foundation upon which to stand and proclaim the truth or a restful place amid the turmoil of the world. In the opening reflection, David Gray provides an analysis of the meaning and reality of Black culture questioning its existence. This may appear to be a strange beginning to a conversation about religious experience, but as the opening chapter unfolds this question forms the backdrop to an answer that assists Black Americans in finding their place in this country, a place of centuries of struggle and failure: that place is the Catholic Church, Her truth and Her traditional forms of worship forming a true and authentic culture.

Each of the authors presents a unique perspective on the importance of their traditional Catholic faith in assisting them in responding to the realities of all that life brings to us. Arlena Brown speaks to the importance of the Traditional Latin Mass in strengthening her marriage, the bond as husband and wife, and providing a faith-filled and generous community of like-minded faithful to support and sustain them. Eric Phillips speaks eloquently of the power of the intellect to illuminate and expand our faith. The works and words of the Fathers, the beauty of Sacred Scripture, the dogma and doctrine of the faith assisted in Mr. Phillip's deepening his bond with Holy Mother Church. Moreover, in his reflections, he offers the wise insight that manifest growth and time will resolve the debates between the Traditional Latin Mass and the Novus Ordo Missae. In her honest and personal reflections, Geraldine Precil speaks about her long association with the Latin Mass and her understanding of its depth, beauty, and transcendence. She also addresses the reality of authentic fruit borne of the Traditional sacraments and teachings of the Church that comes as much through wisdom, experience, and humility as it does from the grace of the sacraments. We must actively receive that which is freely given to us through the Church's teachings, practice, and prayer. Jackson Pickney articulates truths that need to be spoken but is often silenced for fear of rejection or hostile attack. He reminds the reader of the rich contribution of Black Americans to this country during much more adverse periods of racial segregation and hatred. Yet, the voices of Black conservatives who offer the sage and age-old advice of self-determination, hard work, discipline, and faith are silenced because the narrative of the Black man in America is about victimhood, blaming, and shaming others. This work concludes with the personal experiences of David

Gray himself. He speaks of the struggle of responding to what Black society demanded of him and the freedom that Holy Mother Church gave him to be who God called him to be. Through the "ritual, the order, the form, the silence, the reverence of Holy Mass", Mr. Gray was able to truly find himself and, in that discovery, experience the peace that only comes through the truth.

On a personal note, the reading of these reflections reminds me that I am neither crazy nor alone. There are so few Black Catholic priests, and at least to my knowledge, even fewer who are involved in the apostolic work of the traditional Mass and sacraments. There have been times when the experience of alienation and loneliness was extremely profound as I grappled with the specter of racism both from without and within the Church and hostility in the Church because of my love and appreciation for the traditional sacraments. As the authors in this book, the only option that is left to us straddling different worlds, responding to different expectations of identity and community is to choose the only identity that matters and the only community that saves: Our Lord Jesus Christ and His spouse, Holy Mother Church. Regardless of race, this is the only choice for the peace of the world and the salvation of all mankind!

God's Prodigal People

A measurable amount of opinion has been spent on responding to a 2019 Pew Research Polling of 8,660 Black adults (6% of whom identified as Catholic), which found that 46% of those who had been raised Catholic (cradle Catholics) no longer identify as such, 19% of those Black cradle Catholics have become unaffiliated with any religion and 24% have converted to Protestantism. This contrasts with the 81% of Black Americans who were raised in a Protestant denomination and still identify as Protestant (1% of those raised in a Protestant denomination now identify as Catholic).

There is very little benefit gained in continuing with extracting the Pew Research poll for insight about cradle Catholics, given the insignificant number of Catholics, altogether, who participated in the poll (of the 6% many were also Black immigrants from Africa or the Caribbean) but something can be said about the overall findings of the poll, which merited a very typical response from the political-left wing of Black American Catholics.

Black Americans have long been staunchly and faithfully Democratic, both politically and socially. Justin Nortey noted in his analysis that 91% (more than nine-in-10) Black Protestants voted for Joseph R. Biden in 2020, "as did seven-in-10" Black American religiously- unaffiliated "nones" (71%). Therefore, it reflected well in the 2019 Pew Research Poll that found that the 84% of Black Protestants (85% Black cradle Catholics) of those who identified as Democrats also attended religious services less often than the 10% of those who identified as Republican or lean Republican; they were also less likely to state that religion is very important in their lives (58% to 60%), more likely to state that abortion should be legal in all or most cases (72% to 42%), and more likely to state that homosexuality should be accepted in society (66% to 42%). Therefore, when the results of this poll were used by people such as Rev. Bryan Massingale (who identifies himself as a Black Gay Priest), and Alejandra Molina, to push a narrative that Black Catholics want a Church that addresses racism, racism justice, anti-Whiteness, and to hear sermons that speak to "distinctive struggles of Black people in America," these were not conclusions based on reality.

There is no evidence that any substantial number of faithful Black Catholics (i.e., those obedient and faithful to Church precepts and dogma) put society's imaginary race construct before their faith. Moreover, this type of unfortunate reaction was rooted in the flawed idea that the Church should be formed by the people and their truth, rather than that the people are the ones who should be formed by the Church and Her Truth.

Rather than being an indictment of the failures of the Church in not conforming Herself to the world, what the Pew Research poll truly is, is an indictment of the Church and Her failure to form and orient all the people of society to Christ Jesus. Regarding Black cradle Catholics, there should not be a world where 46% of them found something greater than the Sacrament of the Holy Eucharist, or such a small number of them believing that weekly worship at the liturgy of the Holy Mass substantially contributes to their salvation.

In the Beginning

It was not always this way. Whether the numbers indicate that we are in a period of decline or not for Black American Catholics, we do know that it is not an era of substantial growth and conversions, such as we witnessed from 1940 to 1975 when the Black Catholic population in the United States grew from 300,000 to nearly one million. Amazingly, the most explosive growth in the Catholic Church among Black Americans occurred during the heights of legalized discrimination against Blacks, while the traditional Latin Mass was the ordinary liturgy. According to the United States Conference of Catholic Bishops, there are an estimated three million Black Catholics in the United States; about 750,000 belong to culturally Black Catholic parishes. Also included in this number are an undetermined number of immigrants from the continent of Africa and the Caribbean.

There was such explosive growth in the Catholic Church among Black Americans in just thirty-five years and during a time of intense discrimination, bigotry, and racism. Yet, during the past fifty years in a post-segregation society and while the Novus Ordo liturgy allows for liturgical abuses and insertions that we have been told are more attractive to Black Americans, there has not been a growth of Black Catholics matching the increase of population among Black Americans. This phenomenon is something that demands an answer.

According to the Gospel of John, near the Feast of Dedication, the Jews began pressing Jesus to answer the question directly about whether He was the Messiah or not; "tell us plainly," so He did, saying, "The Father and I are one." Have you ever begged someone to tell you something and when they did, you got mad at them for telling you what you were begging them to? Such was the case with the Jews who "picked up rocks to stone Him," and after Jesus began asking them questions about why they didn't believe the evidence that proves He is God, they tried to arrest Him; and then something amazing happened.

Life is full of red herrings and unnecessary details; many of which just overcomplicate and cloud our vision from seeing the answer that, oftentimes, stands right before us. Sometimes we need to return to the beginning of the thing, so that we might remember that first spark of love, and remember what and why we first believed. In this case, the text informs us, after they tried to arrest Jesus, "He went back across the Jordan to the place where John first baptized, and there he remained. Many came to him and said, "John performed no sign, but everything John said about this man was true." And many there began to believe in him." That is, they returned to the beginning, and they remembered, and they believed.

Race (as a multifaceted skin tone) and color-line constructs are not real. There are no species of humans that are known by the accident of skin color. There is no real thing called a 'Black community'; rather, that is a political assignment, just as the nomenclature 'African-American' was. Instead, what we have are millions of people and families throughout the United States with various social, religious, political, education, and economic alignments, and because many of these so-called 'Blacks' are predominantly and historically grouped in many of the same cities and regions, we find various common intersections of religion, politics, wealth, education, and etcetera among them.

We might deign to posit that these intersections are evidence of there being a 'Black' community or a 'Black' culture, and I will address that opinion shortly, but for now, it suffices to imagine as if Black Americas were a monolithic community. What is the faith of these people? Who were they in the beginning? That we should imagine such a thing is important in the face of people imagining that we can use the findings of a Pew Research poll to speak of such a monolithic Black race of people and inform the Catholic Church about what it needs to change to encounter these people.

The Feast Day of Saint Augustine of Hippo, September 8, 1565, was a Saturday in the Julian calendar; seventeen years before Pope Gregory XIII would issue his papal bull, *Inter gravissias,* to announce the reform of calendars in Catholic Christendom. On that day, the roots of so-called Black Catholicism were established on the shores of La Florida as both free and slave, man, woman, and child assembled with the other settlers who arrived on the ships captained by Pedro Menéndez de Avilés, carrying around 800 Spaniards. They all gathered on that day and many more to come as Franciscan Father Franciso Lopez Mendoza Grajales celebrated the pre-Tridentine Roman rite liturgy (the Roman missal would not be reformed until 1570).

In the late summer of 1619, the remaining 30 of an original 350 Kimbundu-speaking men and women from the Kingdon of Ndongo in Central Africa who had been captured and enslaved after infighting with local Imbangala mercenaries and Portuguese colonizers, were stolen off the ship San Juan Bautista, which was on course to Vera Cruz, Mexico from Luanda, Angola. Before the

San Juan Bautista arrived, English pirates aboard the White Lion and Treasurer attacked the ship and "stole around 60 of the surviving" Kingdom of Ndongo people and sailed for Virginia and were sold to the Virginia Company official in exchange for supplies. These were the first slaves from the continent of Africa who were sold off into English-speaking and predominately Protestant North America. It is not known how many worked as indentured servants versus lifelong slaves.

Around seventy years later, the first underground railroad for fleeing slaves was established en route to Saint Augustine. In 1693, King Charles II of Spain promulgated a royal decree granting asylum in Florida to any English-based slave who converted to Catholicism and served for four years in the colonial militia. Due to the growth in their Black Catholic militia, in 1738 Governor Montiano ordered the construction of Gracia Real de Santa Teresa de Mose (also called, Fort Mose), to be established as a northern defense fort for the settlement of Saint Augustine. Fort Mose was the first legally sanctioned settlement of free Blacks in North America, and at the center of the village was a Catholic church in which Black cradle Catholics and new Black Catholic converts worshipped in the traditional Latin Mass.

Fort Mose was just two miles north of Saint Augustine and by 1573 more Franciscan missionaries arrived and had established the Mission of Nombre de Dios in 1587, which was on the northern outskirts of Saint Augustine. Other Franciscan monasteries and chapels were also erected around the developing area. Missionaries from the Society of Jesus (Jesuits) had previously arrived to convert native Americans in Florida but had left in 1571. Although there were secular priests also in the area, the predominant spiritual influence upon Black Catholics at this time and on other converts here was Franciscan. Unlike most religious orders of the time, the Franciscans did not have their own liturgical rite but exclusively celebrated the Roman rite.

The creation of Fort Mose was also a reaction to a growing British presence in southern Georgia and the threat posed by their alliance with the native Indian Muscogulge peoples. Here, Patrick Riordan notes, "The town of Mose became home to 75 to 100 former English slaves and the first self-governing community of free African Americans in North America." Prominent figures at Fort Mose include Francisco Menendez, who was an escaped slave from Carolina. It was Francisco who was put in charge of new arrivals at the first Black Catholic settlement. Fort Mose continued its service to Spain and the underground railroad until 1763 when Spain ceded East Florida to the British in the Treaty of Parish. Thereafter, most of the area's Black residents, numbering over 3,000 (about 75% of whom were escaped slaves), emigrated to Cuba where they resettled and continued their Catholic faith journey under Spanish rule.

Freedom and Faith
In the beginning, those who are called 'Black' in North America always associated Catholicism with Freedom. They also associated it with defending their faith and their freedom against outside attacks. It was not about skin color for them, because some Spaniards were just as pale as some of the Brits. On the contrary, for them, freedom meant entering a whole new world of catechesis, Baptism, confession, language spoken in Latin, mystery, ritual, worshipping in the same direction that the priest celebrant was facing, and the Holy Eucharist. It meant not only freedom for yourself, but your entire family who would be numbered among the Catholic families baptized into the faith.

Venerable Pierre Toussaint was a slave in two countries but was never a slave in his heart, and in every way he was Catholic.

Although he attended the traditional Latin Mass daily at Saint Peter's Church on Barclay Street in New York City, he never asked for a Church to speak to his temporary difficulties or for a Church to be more like the finite world. Proudly Haitian, born there in 1766, Pierre resolves the question of how one can be happily from one place but also headed to another to be happy eternally. Being his full Black self or full Haitian self was not the Catholic ideal for Pierre, but being fully at the service of his neighbor was. For, while he was here, his life was devoted to freedom through charity. After being granted his freedom, he even took the surname of Toussaint, perhaps in honor of Toussaint Louverture, a prominent general in the Haitian revolution.

If Venerable Toussaint's charity was just for Catholics or Blacks, we would have something to hold against him, but he even loved Marie, his master's widow, until she died in 1807. He used the money he earned not only to give his wife (Juliette Noel, also a Haitian), her sister, and other slaves freedom from slavery but he also adopted his niece, Euphemia, after her mother's death and educated her in French and English. Euphemia later died from tuberculosis. Pierre and Juliette used their Manhattan home to give refuge and education to orphaned children. They also nursed people who were suffering from yellow fever. They gave generously to the Oblate Sisters of Providence for their school in New York established exclusively to educate Black girls.

Venerable Pierre Toussaint found freedom in charity, again, something so counter-cultural, that it can only be through the belief that you are a eucharistic person; that your life is both an offering and a sacrifice; not for your sake, but, rather, for the glory of Him who lives in you. Asked why he did not retire and enjoy his accumulated wealth, Pierre responded, "I have enough for myself, but if I stop working I have not enough for others." Pierre and Juliette died in 1853 and 1851, respectively.

We should not be asking how we can make Catholic worship more palatable or how to make our homilies more titillating to the ears or what our Bishops can do to appear to be more relatable to current suffering. Rather, what we should do is point to people like Venerable Pierre Toussaint who teaches what a life sustained by the Holy Eucharist looks like; far above earthly concerns, but deeply in love with each of us.

Another French-speaking Haitian who demonstrated the power of faith and freedom was Elizabeth Lange (c. 1789 – February 3, 1882). We do not know exactly when or where she was born, but it is presumed that based on her education, she hailed from an affluent Haitian family that fled to Cuba near the time the revolution began in 1791, and in her early twenties made her way to Baltimore, Maryland in 1813, by way of Charleston, South Carolina and Norfolk, Virginia.

Without any excuses for being a woman, living in a state where slavery was legal, where people were being kidnapped into slavery, and it was illegal to educate slaves, Elizabeth Lange leveraged her own money, home, and friendships to provide free education to as many Black children as she could, and when she had done all that she could do, the providence of God provided a way for her to continue her work. In 1829, with the guidance of Father James Nicholas Joubert, a member of the Society of the Priests of Saint Sulpice, Elizabeth, and three other women pronounced their solemn vows of obedience to the Archbishop of Baltimore, James Whitfield; Elizabeth became the foundress and first superior of the Oblate Sisters of Providence; taking the name of Mary.

Another French-speaking Mother Superior, Henriette Delille, was born in New Orleans on March 11, 1813. There is any number of concerning things about Henriette's life before her reversion experience. She was born under questionable circumstances with her mother and the other women in her family never marrying but having relations with various wealthy White men (i.e., concubinage). She may have even found herself groomed for such a life, having given birth outside of marriage to two sons who died before the age of three. DeLille owned a slave named Betsy, whom she did not free at any point during her life. Some might even be concerned that after her mother, Marie-Josèphe, suffered a nervous breakdown, DeLille provided for her care and then sold the rest of her mother's assets to use in establishing her congregation of Sisters of the Presentation.

Yet, what is substantially redeeming about Venerable Henriette DeLille's life was that it demonstrates clear evidence of someone on the path of decrease so that Christ might increase in them. She voluntarily chooses a life of suffering and service. As an octoroon (i.e., 7/8th White), like her brother Jean, she could have passed as White but chose to identify as Black at a time in Louisiana when legal discrimination, bigotry, and racism against Blacks were openly practiced and flaunted. Even Catholics in the Church rejected her application to join an existing religious order, not allowing her to wear a religious habit (i.e., specific clothing for consecrated life), and required her to make private, not public, vows of consecration.

Venerable Henriette DeLille welcomed such suffering and humiliation so that she might be at the full service of the sick, poor, and uneducated. Such saintly behavior only happens when a Christian believes they are not suffering for their own sake, but, rather, for the sake of Him who suffered and was humiliated first and for our sake. The freedom that comes from believing that our life belongs to Him who gave us His life for free is deeper than any ocean and sets in us a fire that is hotter than any sun.

The lives of holy people are liturgical; that is, they are eucharistic (i.e., for the people's good, self-giving, sacrificial, oriented to Christ, and present and visiting those in need). In this way, the lives of holy people remind us of the traditional liturgies of the Catholic Church which are naturally resistant to the priest or people making worship about themselves or catering to the entertainment factor. The life of Servant of God Julia Greeley (1833/1848 – 1918) is a perfect example of how one might model their life to be a type of liturgy in the world.

Born into legal slavery and freed by Missouri's Emancipation Proclamation Act of 1865, Julia left that state of life illiterate and with just one eye and eventually made her way from Saint Louis, Missouri, where she worked as a cook and nanny for Dr. Paul G. Robinson and his wife Lina, to Denver, Colorado in the late 1870s, following the Gilpin family who was related to the Robinsons. William Gilpin was the first territorial governor of Colorado, and it was his wife, Julia (formerly Julia Pratte Dickerson), who encouraged Julia to convert to Catholicism in Denver.

It was in Denver, Coloration, where Julia Greely spent all her remaining days living a life modeled after the liturgy of the Catholic Mass. When Julia was not at daily Mass or working as a housemaid or loving children, she could be found walking through the city, visiting its many fire stations to evangelize about the Sacred Heart of Jesus and assisting poor families with their needs. Although Julia was poorer than many of the people she was assisting, Julia demonstrated a humble and unselfish charity by delivering the items people needed under the cover of night and by way of dark alleys. Julia also joined the Secular Franciscan Order in 1901 and remained active in it until her death. Servant of God Julia Greeley lived her life for other people.

Indeed, Catholics have a two-thousand-year history of seeing work needing to be done and doing it, and Catholics have always been at our best when everything was against us because we knew that God is not on their side, but, rather, truly dwelling on us and with us. When you know this and you believe this, the Catholic faith is not something you leave. Rather, it is something you dig deeper into and cleave to. The Catholic faith has the truth (namely a person named Jesus Christ) whom we do not have to apologize for or try to change and make more acceptable. All we must do is take up our cross and follow Him, and all these other things will be added unto us.

To be sure, carrying one's own cross will never be easy and it comes included with sacrifice. Enduring fortitude and sacrificial love are just two Christian virtues that are antithetical to a post-Christian society that only evangelizes and accepts what is easy and non-sacrificial.

From the moment he was born into slavery until the day he died from complications of a heat stroke during a Chicago heatwave, Venerable Father Augustus Tolton (April 1, 1854 – July 9, 1897) knew what his purpose in life was and stayed the course to the end. In the face of prejudice, envy, bigotry, racism, discrimination, jealousy, marginalizing, segregation, and every other thing that comes out of the heart of man, Tolton stayed the course, and when he could not anymore, he continued his way in another diocese until his death.

One essential commonality among Venerable Pierre Toussaint, Venerable Henriette DeLille, Venerable Father Augustus Tolton, Servant of God Mother Mary Lange, and Servant of God Julia Greeley is that all of them were in love with the traditional Latin Mass. Furthermore, not one of them thought it was the Catholic Church that needed to change. Not one of them tried to change the liturgy to make it more culturally Black. Not one of them tried to change the liturgical music to make it more culturally Black. Not one of them tried to change anything whatsoever about the Church. Rather, they worked day and night to bring Christ into the world through their vocation of love. Not one of them thought that there was something salvific about their skin color, or because they were descendants from Haiti or the continent of Africa they needed to be fully Haitian to be fully Catholic, or that they were required to view the world through race constructs. Not one of them thought they were being fully Catholic by being Haitian or Creole or Black American.

On the contrary, like every saint before them, they believed that they were a eucharistic people who were following the call to be in the world who they have received through the liturgy. This is what it means to be truly free in Christ.

The greatest tragedy and embarrassment in the Catholic Church today is the idea that we need to turn these humble souls into affirmative-action saints, by having them declared "santo subito" (saint now, by popular acclamation), thereby circumventing the ordinary processes, miracles, and investigations. What a complete disgrace it would be for Toussaint, DeLille, Tolton, Lang, and Greeley to have an asterisk placed next to their names for having been canonized through a special process, due to their earthly skin color. Why should these holy people be turned into charity cases by those who need some sort of race-based affirmation? At particular points in their earthly lives, Toussaint, DeLille, Tolton, Lang, and Greeley were all assisted by Catholics who prayed, promoted and sacrificed for them to continue their calling. Who are we not to continue those prayers, promotions, and sacrifices for them, now that they are not with us? I do not know at what time hard work, unceasing prayer, and enduring patience started being antithetical to being culturally Black, but such a mindset needs to stay away from tarnishing the heroic virtues of Toussaint, DeLille, Tolton, Lang, and Greeley.

There is No Balm in Gilead
The Prophet Jeremiah's question, "Is there no balm in Gilead, no healer there?" at first sight seems contradictory, until we read the

verse as a rhetorical device. For, throughout the sacred Scriptures, Gilead is known as a place where one might acquire a healing balm. On the contrary, what Jeremiah is responding to here is the blind habit the people of Jerusalem had of turning to the world, rather than to God for true healing. In their obstinacy and refusal to convert, they forsook God and turned away from their glory in pursuit of "useless things."

it is today in this post-Christian society that we live in, where every sin has a worldly solution attached to it. Every sin has a legislative agenda, public policy, political party platform, hashtag, march on Washington, D.C., theory, program, corporate training, and social media cancelation (public shaming), to address and fix it. It has gotten to the point that people are publicly calling for sins, such as racism, to end; as if man has it in his capabilities and purview to do something that Christ Jesus did not even do away with on the Cross; as if man has it in his power and purview to rebirth the world through an immaculate reconception. Human hubris has no limit.

A post-Christian society is also a post-truth society. Therefore, in a post-truth society, we expect people to be inclined to believe the lies of Satan, to live a life based upon those lies, and, thereby, inclined to seek out the balm of Gilead, rather than the Sacraments of the Catholic Church.

One of the most unfortunate areas where this tendency to pursue the balm of Gilead plays out is in predominantly Black communities in the United States.

Throughout history, the three building blocks of a healthy and sustainable society were marriage, morals, and education. Societies in which men and women are given in marriage and have children, where there is an enforceable divine moral law, and people have the tools to improve their environment, and the means to provide for the family, are societies that can be sustained longer than societies that do not have these building blocks in place. People who have families have something to protect and people whose values are rooted in divine revelation believe they have a duty and a calling to protect what God has gifted them with. Today, we could also include other metrics, such as health, employment, debt, and homeownership other indicators of a healthy society.

Yet, unfortunately, in nearly every statistical category of human development and sustainability, predominately Black communities in the United States are far behind other groups. For example, in those areas in which Catholic moral and social values have something specific to say, Black women are the only group who have a higher divorce rate than marriage rate.

In education, high school dropout rates have been steadily decreasing for Black Americans since 2010 and are lower than Hispanics, but Black single mothers are the most likely to drop out of high school, and so we find Black women leading with 64% of their children born into unwed families and also leading in the poverty rate at 48.1%.

Given the increase in interracial marriages, especially in larger cities with more affluent and educated Blacks, it is difficult to contrast race versus race constructs, but in 2017, there was still a 30.1 percentage point gap between Black and White homeownership, which is wider than it was when race-based discrimination was allowed by law. The percentage rate of home ownership by native Black Americans is near the same rate as first-generation immigrants from the continent of Africa and the Caribbean islands, which is an indictment against Black Americans who have been here for several generations since legal home ownership home loan has been outlawed.

In 1900, the United States Census Bureau found 8.8 million Black Americans, which accounted for 11.6% of the total population of 76.3 million. One hundred years later, the census found 34.6

million Black Americans who accounted for 12.3 percent of the total population of 282.2 million. In 2020, 41.1million Black Americans accounted for 12.4% of the total U.S. population of 329.5 million. These numbers inform us that from 1900 to 2000 the total U.S. population grew by 271%, but the Black American population only grew by 38%. In that same period, the population of White Americans increased by 185.4% (75,994,575 / 216,900,000)

The fact that the percentage of Black Americans in this country has not significantly increased over time cannot be completely explained by higher infant mortality rates among Black children, the Black communities' embrace of Margaret Sanger's (Planned Parenthood) birth control movement, and, later, their embracing of Planned Parenthood's surgical abortion genocide, with Black women disproportionately aborting their children at significantly higher rates than White women (38% to 33%).

Although artificial birth control and the Black abortion genocide are significant contributors to the stunting of the Black American population, other immorality factors t also play a role in the fact that Black Americans have historically had significantly lower birth rates than other people in the United States. Married women have substantially higher birth rates than single women and never wed women, which affects Black women whose marriage rates dropped from 61% in 1960 (Whites were at 74%) to 32% in 2008 (Whites, 61%).

Outside of factors concerning immorality but still part of the social responsibility to human development, highly educated women are more likely to have bigger families than women with high school or less education. Globally, women who belong to cultures that promote larger families (e.g., Pacific Islander and Hispanic) have more children than cultures that do not (e.g., Black, Asian, White).

In specific concern to Black Americans, imagine if they were to embrace the moral and social teachings of the Catholic Church, which promotes sacramental and permanent marriage, large families, and education. Everything else Black Americans have been doing in this country, from embracing Protestantism, to the pseudo-religion of political party loyalty, materialism, and secularism has failed them. The proof is in the numbers.

The answer to the problem of low Black-American birth rates, high divorce rates, the abortion genocide, and everything else that has contributed to Black Americans remaining a small minority in a country that many of their ancestors built is embracing Catholicism; in particular, traditional and orthodox Catholic praxis. Traditional Catholicism is the balm that can heal all people, and the sick are those who are in most need of it.

The Race, Culture, Grievance & Essentialism Myths
In 2022, the so-called Black culture is a myth. There is no such thing as a Black culture in the traditional sense of culture because there is no such thing as the Black community in the traditional sense of community. If you do not have a community, you do not have a culture. If we can expose this myth, there is hope that Black Americans will embrace a proven 2,000year-old Catholic culture and emigrate from the Black race construct created by racists and race essentialists to the human race created by God.

The term 'Black community is merely a historical idea found dead since integration, but race essentialists still love to bandy around because it gives them leverage and value. Before integration, there was a multi-layered pre-Civil War Black culture, and then there was a multi-layered pre-integration Black Culture, but today this is just a political term, used by political agents to push the color-line myth (which reinforces the Black culture myth) as if there are some dark-skinned people in the United States who all think alike. Granted, the evidence of Black Americans voting Democrat in the 90th percentile for decades is evidence that the color-line myth has been embraced by those who wanted to embrace it.

Historically, culture has always been able to be identified as having five marks: (1) traditions (e.g., the sacraments of the people – the things and values and beliefs that made them who they are – their national story), (2) a means/mechanism to pass down those traditions (e.g., elders and their stories, rituals, initiation rites), (3) a visible community (they know where to find each other and others can find them as well), (4) a distinct language (not always tongue or dialect, but also a particular way to speak of things), and (5) something they are uniquely known to produce well (e.g., Indian spices, German bread and pianos, Italian wine, Swiss cheese and chocolate, pre-integration Black Jazz).

Concerning culture, two things should be made clear. The first is that on both micro and macro levels, culture can be found anywhere, but what is present there may not always be a 'full' or 'complete' culture. Nations, families, companies, teams, and neighborhoods may all have a culture and within them, there may also be various sub-cultures. Second, the larger the group, the longer that a full culture takes to develop within them; a hundred years typically is long enough for a full culture to develop on a national level. Third, full cultures need a religion (something greater than the individual selfhood to believe in) and sacred history/texts (could also be government laws) that clearly define the community and roles and rules therein. Fourth, culture should never be romanticized as consisting of only the good and beautiful. Culture also carries with it harmful things within each of those five marks.

The idea that race is equivalent to culture is a modern innovation that is rooted in the sins of objectification and pride. The sacred religious texts of Judaism, Christianity, and Islam are all mute about skin color being equivalent to race or ethnicity. In this context, the only concern of the sacred texts is where a person is from and from whom they descend. Even the Book of Pylon, which dates from Egypt's New Kingdom period (between 1570 BC and 1544 BC) posits only four different groups of people: "Reth" (Egyptians), "Aamu" (Asiatics), "Nehesu" (Nubians), and "Themehu" (Libyans).

Rather, it was not until the moral justification for the Transatlantic slave trade was needed that a new classification of the human species was developed. If one group of people are intrinsically (by their very nature) inferior and predisposed to bondage and chattel slavery, it could be morally justifiable for a group who is racially refined and cultured to enslave them.

Therefore, it was necessary for the terms the "White race" and "White people' to enter the human lexicon, so that race was no longer based upon where one is from, but on what they look like, which equated to their natural intellectual superiority or inferiority. Later, being 'White' or being 'Black' also became associated with how one viewed the world and interacted with others so that a person could appear to be of the Black race but act as belonging to the White race.

Nearly all societies have necessarily developed myths and created legends to explain their superiority and have passed down sacraments from one generation to the next to reinforce nationalism, patriotism, supremacy, and psychosis into the identity of the people. Aside from the Nation of Islam teaching that the White race is a bunch of inbred, blond, blue-eyed, White devils who were without morals or compassion, Black Americans are the only people who have been trained to not believe they are better than anyone else. They are the only people who have been given sacraments such as Black History Month and pseudo-religions such as

Black Lives Matter to reinforce historical grievances, and Marxist pseudo-religions such as Kwanzaa to teach them to look outside of their nation to discover the greatness of a different group of people who share their same skin color.

One of the oldest myths used by cultures to explain their superiority over the dark-skinned races is the interpreted 'Curse of Ham'. There has been a great deal of scholarship in recent years concerning whether racism can be located outside the framework of European modernity. David M. Goldenberg would like us to move away from the Jewish Talmudic exegesis and postbiblical texts which equate the term 'Ham' in Hebrew with 'blackness' so that we might place the real blame on the Muslims for perverting Noah's curse on Canaan. For his part, Haroon Bashir, in Black Excellence and the Curse of Ham: Debating Race and Slavery in the Islamic Tradition, admits that although the story of Noah's curse is not founded in the Qur'an, it is a story that has been transmitted via Islamic literature and used as justification for anti-dark-skinned racism "throughout the transatlantic slave-trade." Bashir's most interesting conclusion is that the rabid focus of Jewish and Western scholars on Islamic texts has not only been overgeneralized but was political in nature, in an attempt to take the attention from White supremacy by pointing to the Arab/Muslim as the real racist.

This history of justified racism within the various European and Arab traditions only makes the historical appeal of Black Americans to these same cultures quite remarkable but given all the inner-class-supremacy and color lines within the Black American community itself (Black Catholics not excluded), all we are left with is a realization of the hypocrisy found in the human condition. That is, even without a color-line, peoples and nations have always found the justification they needed to subjugate other peoples and nations. In Germany, for instance, the Nazis could not always merely look at a person and identify them as a being a Jew; further investigation of their home, relationships, and the family tree was required. The Kosovo War, The Troubles, and the Civil War in Chad were some of the most recent deadly conflicts that were fought by people who were indistinguishable from each other in appearance.

Indeed, the propensity of the natural human to harm others, based upon one's faith in the myths of superiority, had long existed before color-line racism. On the contrary, the color-line only made hate and prejudice at-first-sight easier. It made hate and prejudice mere exercises in objectification. The idea that I do not have to investigate why I am different than another, based upon things we might discover through conversation and prolonged investigation, that I can just hate them based upon appearance is a type of uncivilized and sub-human behavior pattern that should always be exposed and deemed unacceptable by all civilized people. Outside of the love of God, humans in their natural condition will always find cause to hate each other, but in Christ, humans, raised to their supernatural dignity, will always find a reason to love each other.

Nevertheless, we are left to contend with this harmful redefinition and classification of the human people along color lines. The so-called Black American is now struggling for the third time to create a culture while being absorbed and assimilated into a broader and more mature American culture. We also find the Black American Catholic caught in a third tension; of not only being called to live an authentically Catholic life but also to live according to the precepts of what it means to be a culturally Black American. Given that the ideologies of the three tensions are incompatible with the others, at some point in time, the Black Catholic must decide whether they will live this life as a Catholic in America or a Black person in America. These two things are mutually exclusive.

The pigeonholing of a group of people, not based upon their lived cultural experience, but rather upon the accident of skin color, not only diminishes their full human value but also stagnates their growth as a people because they are being forced to cling to the false idea that skin color and citizenship are marks of culture, which they never have been. Rather, it has always been within the complexity of the accidents of skin tone and citizenry that we have found a variety of cultures and sub-cultures.

Alongside skin tone and citizenship being determinative factors and prerequisites of who is and who is not a culturally Black person in America is the myth that to be a culturally Black American one must faithfully subscribe to the ideological culture of post-integration Black Americana as we see it developed today. The cultural traditions of Black Americana, that is, the things that define them and they must preserve, are two: (1) the historical grievance; that is, the belief that Black Americans today are personally and effectively impacted by the harm done to some/many Blacks and their descendants since the Transatlantic slave trade, and (2) political allegiance to the Democrat party, which has found Black Americans consistently and uncritically voting for the Democrat party in or near the 90th percentile, a phenomenal accomplishment of a political party – the type of which we have not seen anywhere else in the world at any point in history.

Before the ending of legal slavery, the Black American culture was divided into three sub-cultures: the Black slave plantation culture and a Black freed/escaped Black slave culture (paid laborers), and a Black bourgeoisie (land holding, voting, slave holding, intellectual, and Black Protestant preacher class). Then after the Civil War, the Black slave plantation culture emigrated into the Black freed and escape labor class and either remained in the south to work the fields and send their children to the new Black universities or emigrated to the northern and western states. Together, the labor class worked to establish a real and full culture and aspired for their children to make it into the Black bourgeoisie class after they had graduated from university. This arrangement between the labor class and the Black bourgeoise was working well for a century until the latter, always wanting to emulate their 'betters', undermined the Black middle class in America by selling them on the idea of integration; calling it their civil right. And from that moment on, the Black middle class has found itself in the position of desiring the community they lost, yet all the while being absorbed and assimilated into the American culture.

Returning to the second mark of culture (the means to pass down traditions), cultural traditions are not real and effective traditions if they are not passed down from one generation to the next. Regarding the historical grievance, it is a tradition that has been passed down and assigned through the story, song, and holy days for over a half-century. Black mothers teach their sons that they must fear the police and White people; telling the world that they go into a state of anxiety every time their husbands and sons leave the home. The retelling of stories about the 1921 Tulsa massacre, the Tuskegee experiment (1932 –1972), the assassination and imprisonment of Black leaders, segregation, Jim Crow, slavery, and lately the deaths of Black men and women at the hands of law enforcement. These stories are enshrined in the federal Martin Luther King Jr. holiday, where Blacks are called to sing the song 'We Shall Overcome', even while in 2022 there are not any legal obstacles in place for Black Americans to overcome and Black History Month where children are forced to endure 28 days of indoctrination of the historic grievance tradition.

Concerning the other three marks of culture, distinct language, visible community, and something they produce, there is no clear evidence that these things exist on a national level. The reason being is primarily that there is no such thing as a distinct Black

American community in the traditional sense. If there is no community, there is no full culture. If we were to find the Black cooperative communities, the type that we still find today among the various Chinese, Indian, Bosnian, and Arab communities, and with pre-integration Black communities, then we could be empowered to claim that Blacks Americans still do have a visible community.

On the contrary, what we find is that there are about 11 million independent Black families (married and cohabitating) scattered across the United States, but predominately situated in urban areas. Now, within these pockets across America, we might find within them those community bonds and praxis (both positive and negative). We might find therein a particular language, dialect, or a way they uniquely speak about things. We might also find that they are uniquely producing something that they export or that people come to them to experience (e.g., food, jazz, hip-hop, breakdancing). Unfortunately, on the national scale, language, community, and product are only present in a culture that Black Americans are being absorbed and assimilated into, which is the American culture that believes in only three things: (1) consumption, (2) disposal, and (3) self-deification.

Establishing a culture after such global ignorance and psychosis have not only emerged and become normalized but now have legal protections, is impossible. We have countless generations around the world now believing that something so accidental as skin color and hair grade is equivalent to something as complex as culture and ethnicity. For, if race is as basic as something accidental, insignificant, and in no way connected to the five marks of a full culture, as skin tone is, then the higher ideals of faith, values, and principles could never have the higher aims of significance and essence.

Yet, herein lies the permanent disability of speaking about race and culture within the lie that one's skin color is their race and the determinative accident which speaks to which culture one belongs to. Truly, culture in America is only skin deep and is why those who would be happy to speak of themselves as Catholic and belonging to the full culture, which is Catholic, are forced to specify and preface that their culture is also Black and then have to even add the additional term of 'Traditional', given the loss that Catholic culture and identity has suffered since the Second Vatican Council. This is truly a miserable state where in polite and popular society the term 'Catholic' means nothing axiomatic on its own, and the term 'Black' should not mean anything regarding who a person is.

In every society, there are competing groups who are at stark odds with the others in a war over the control of ideas, words, and definitions, because those three things shape law, policy, and who the people in the society aspire to be. Once you direct the aspiration of the people, that is, their idealistic life, you are then able to reinforce that ideal through the cultural sacraments and myths that are passed down from one generation to the next.

In every culture the 'who' is different, but it is always a competition of ideas, words, and definitions, between groups, where one group always has more influence in controlling the narrative than the others. In most Middle Eastern countries, the dominant group is always one of the two main sects of Islam, Sunni or Shi'ite. In most Western countries, the dominant groups are the political parties and the multinational corporations. Post-Monarchism, there remain very few societies today where the Catholic Church is still able to influence their culture in any substantive way that shapes ideas, words, and definitions and makes their way into law, policy, and the idealistic aspiration. Perhaps Poland and Russia are the last countries where the multinational corporations have not supplanted the role that the Catholic or Orthodox Church once had in influencing government.

In the United States, the 'good life' or the 'American dream' aspiration may at one time have been as James Truslow Adams described it in his 1931 bestselling book, Epic America, which was for everyone to have a better, richer, and fuller life with the opportunity for every American according to their ability or achievement. Eventually, that dream was realized by the display of successful consumerism. Today, that dream has turned into the nightmare of disposing of everything that we consume, only to consume more, and to self-deify ourselves along the way by deluding our minds to believe that our ability to display a litany of disposing and consuming is evidence that we are our god.

Underneath the American culture of consumption, disposal, and self-deifying, are various sub-cultures that have their own definitions that intersect with and cross-pollinate with other cultures. There are also groups within each sub-culture that are at war with each other over the control of ideas, words, and definitions within that culture, so that they might shape traditions, myths, and aspirations of the good life.

In the sub-culture of Black America today, there are four competing groups at war for control: (1) The old-guard Black bourgeoise (including the Black Protestant Preacher class), (2) The new-guard Black feminist matriarchy (and their effeminate Black male/LGBT allies), (3) The new Black patriarchy, and (4) The first generation real African/Caribbean Americans (the children of immigrants from Africa the Caribbean islands). Each of these four groups wants to control and define what it means to be Black in America.

In the early decades of the post-integration wave of the new Black culture, well-meaning Black folks, most especially American leftist political activist, Reverend Jesse L. Jackson Sr., convinced White folk to matriculate a third time in how they should address their lessers; they should call them not Negro, or Colored, or Black, but now African-Americans. The first hope of this new nomenclature was that Black folk would embrace Pan-Africanism and become proud of being descendants of the continent where the vast majority of Black American's ancestors were sold by their own people to European multinational corporations and transported to various countries in North and South America. The second hope was that good White folk would come to believe that Black people were just another historical ethnic group in America, such as the "Armenian-Americans, Jewish-Americans, Arab-Americans, and Italian-Americans."

The 1988 African American hoax was all just a PSYOP and a lie from the beginning. It was all just an attempt by Black Protestant politicians, such as Jackson and Rev. Willie Barrow (i.e., race hustlers) to convince the political establishment and corporations that they are the ones who controlled the Black vote. If they could only convince enough people they were allowed to label millions of Black Americans who have nothing substantively in common with the people in African countries and who cannot trace any of their family-tree back to any of the four dozen sovereign nation-states in Africa, but should be rightly spoken of in the same breath as we would speak of people from the country of Armenia or as we speak about cultural Jews, there would be no telling how much the race-baiting and race hustlers like Rev. Jesse L. Jackson Sr., and his ilk could drain out of the wallets of White folk.

It is far outside the purpose of this title to go deep into this hoax or the dirty laundry list of ways by which the Black bourgeoise and Black Protestant preacher class that people like William Edward Burghardt Du Bois, Rev. Dr. Martin Luther King Jr., Senator James E. Clyburn, Rev. Jesse L. Jackson Sr., and countless others have undermined Black America to its death, but it suffices to say that the Black bourgeoise culture of free and affluent Blacks have always been present in e America. From Anthony Johnson, a wealthy Black Angolan slave-holder from early 17th-century Virginia (colony) who won the first American legal case to indefinitely own a human being who had committed no crime, to the membership of the Prince Hall Free & Accepted Masons in the 18th and 19th centuries, to the leadership of the African Methodist Episcopal Church from the late-1700's till the start of post-segregation, to the Niagara Movement, Sigma Pi Phi, Alpha Phi Alpha, Alpha Kappa Alpha, Jack, and Jill International, and The Links Incorporated, the evidence is clear of their being a continuous and well-established full culture that has as its first principle, the emulation of affluent White culture.

Indeed, for the Black bourgeoisie class, the aspiration of all Black people should be to emulate affluent White people. We should straighten our hair like theirs, we should be as light-skinned as possible, we should dress like them, walk like them, speak like them, live where they live, and use their same ideas, words, and definitions, so that when they see us, they might see themselves as their equal and allow us to have a part of their excellence. Integration was the dream realized for the Black bourgeoisie and the death knell for every other Black American.

The war of ideas and definitions that are present in the Black American experience has always been principally guided by a belief found in all cultures that it is in the power of some (the elite) to control the narrative about what it means to be Black in America. In this last decade, the influence of the Black patriarchy shifted from being anchored in the Grand Sessions of Sigma Pi Phi and the Black Protestant pulpits, and now into the matriarchal and ideological Marxist despots of the Black lay political organizer class, which reached its climax in the Black Lives Matter organization.

The daughters of the Black matriarchy took control after the Bourgeoisie dream of integration failed and the American government filled the leadership void left by the Bourgeoisie class who left their local Black communities to go live with their betters in the suburbs. With their leadership, influence, businesses, and care for property values now gone, the government entered the space, and, with it, so did the destructive elements of crack cocaine and drug gang wars; both offering a new form of bondage to the world. The Democrats' economic welfare plot and a new pseudo-religion called the Church of the Democrats found the Black American woman to be a fine specimen to mend broken fences. Urban Black women were inspired to raise their fatherless sons to be allies of Black liberal feminism and to remain absent as Black they now took the lead in the home, school, politics, media, university classrooms, and eventually boardrooms, thereby becoming the dominant influences and definers of what it means to be a Black American.

The only group that holds any measure of influence over the complete dominance of the new-guard Black feminist matriarchy (along with their effeminate Black male/LGBT allies), is the neo-Black patriarchy. Albeit largely found only on social media platforms, this popular and loud consortium of Black men desires to create/restore the Black patriarchy. The most visible figures of this small group include such notable figures as Tariq Nasheed, founder of the Foundational Black America movement (F.B.A.), Kevin Samuels, a popular YouTube personality, and Dr. Umar Johnson, a widely referenced Black orator.

The status of these men in the social media space, rather than the academy, is not to be disvalued. When the hashtag #BLAMEBLACKMEN was indiscriminately shot from the Tweet gun after radical Black liberal feminists like Jemele Hill ranted again about how bad Black men are, we realized how multifaceted and multiplatform the war for ideas, words, and definitions is. The long-term goal of the neo-Black patriarchy is to restore the Black father to the home and the religious space so that a new generation of masculine Black men can return to the academy, politics, and the boardroom, but in the meantime, they must keep putting a band-aid on the daily hurling of knives being thrown at them on the social media platforms.

As sympathetic as I am to their cause, the neo-Black patriarchy is not without critique. Black women have long taken the leadership mantle in local Black communities and historically, it was always the constructs of culture, religion, and legal systems through which the patriarchy in every society was birthed, protected, and preserved. It is deeply peculiar and sad to watch a group of men attempting to build patriarchy in a post-Christian and post-truth society that is impervious to such a tradition.

It is equally peculiar and sad to watch their opponents trying to reassert a Black feminist matriarchy that has already proven to have failed Black America. Failed, not because Black women and their effeminate sons were incapable of leading, but because there was never a door open in the American culture for such a phenomenon. Moreover, the appearance of the neo-Black male intellectual class of people like Ta-Nehisi Coates, Dr. Ibram X. Kendi, and Dr. Marc Lamont Hill carrying water for the radical, pro-abortion, pro-socialist Black feminist cooperative, has been nothing less than what happens at every five-ring circus clown show of emasculation.

While the neo-Black patriarchy of those like Tariq, Samuels, and Johnson would like to move forward with their new vision for Black America, not only have they had to contend with a well-established Black matriarchy that controls every major city, every Protestant Christian domination, public school, and votes nearly unanimously for the Democratic party that has, through legislation and praxis, entrenched the Black matriarchy, they have also been fighting what has been called 'diaspora wars' against the first generation real African/Caribbean Americans.

Given that the fighting for a new Black patriarchy or a reasserting of the matriarchy is grounded in the idea of there being a real historical grievance, that is, the myth that Black Americans today are personally and effectually impacted by the harm done to Blacks and their descendants since the Transatlantic slave trade, it was only natural that there would be hostility between Black Americans versus Blacks of other cultures, who largely and altogether reject the claim that Black Americans are effectually impacted by the historical grievances, and who also take no accountability for any role that any of their own ancestors may have played in profiting from the Transatlantic slave trade.

The first generation real African/Caribbean Americans, many of whom are Catholic, have no interest in assimilating into or being absorbed into the Black American culture, because they believe that it is a lesser, shameful, and failed cultural experience. Many of them are the children of parents who came to this country poor or whose university degree did not translate into a professional career in this country. They witnessed their parents accomplish in just a few decades what over half of Black Americans have not achieved in five generations. In just one generation, they equal home ownership rates and have less debt than most Black Americans. Their children have higher income, higher education, less debt, own more businesses, and have a lower divorce rate than most Black Americans. They are more likely to marry someone who directly descends from their parents' country or a White American than they are a Black American. They have not become absorbed into the American culture of secularism and LGBT inculturation and have largely rejected the Church of the Democrat Party.

Yet, the first generation African/Caribbean Americans know that the color line is real and that despite how much they despise the Black American culture, they also know that society cannot distinguish them based on appearance, nor does society desire to. Therefore, a vocal number of them have entered the social media space to engage in the diaspora war to try to influence ideas, words, and definitions to reinforce the myths and sacraments within their own sub-cultures that they are better than the Black Americans whose parents their ancestors sold to the multinational corporations because they were nothing but criminals, debtors, dregs of society, and the worst Africa had to offer. In fact, they are just like their ancestors, and we are still the best of Africa, and our success in this country proves it.

Conclusion

Over the years, I have tended to give more attention to the bitter brother than to the entitled son or the merciful father from Luke's parable (15: 11-32), simply because I can relate more to the bitter brother's sense of loyalty and fortitude than I can with someone who does not know what he had until he lost it, or with a father who only had sons, but for our purposes here, I would take another look at the entitled son and the merciful father.

From Simon of Cyrene helping Christ Jesus carry His Cross, to Philip evangelizing and Baptizing the Ethiopian Eunuch, to the very early influence of Catholicism in North Africa to Saint Augustine and Fort Mose to the missionary work of Catholic saints and religious orders prior to the Civil War, Christ and His Church have been the clear inheritance of the descendants of the children of the continent of Africa.

There are any number of fingers to point at regarding who is to blame for selling, trading, and buying slaves, or why Catholic bishops did not work harder to evangelize Black Americans, or why did too many Catholics in the United States embrace the societal norms of segregation, discrimination, bigotry, and Jim Crow. Yet, I never heard anyone blame the merciful father for what happened to his son. No one blames the father for not chasing after his son and bringing him back home immediately. On the contrary, we all just talk about how kind, wonderful, and merciful he was that he did not hold it against his entitled son when he did return home. Perhaps the father believed in God's providence; that God would provide for his son, despite his son's choices and circumstances. Perhaps he prayed for his son's return. Perhaps he also prayed that his son would learn his lesson, but that God would also spare him the worst costs of his decisions.

For his part, the entitled son truly believed that he could make his own way; that he could pull himself up by his bootstraps. The thing about rock-bottom conversion experiences is that you know you have fallen to the bottom of the pit and hit the rocks. Hitting rock bottom is not like falling into a sunken space and still trying to find something to hold onto. No, when you hit rock bottom, you know for a fact that you cannot help yourself out of the hole that you are in. So, you turn to someone who can help you. You return to the Jordan River where John the Baptist first told you about Jesus. You return home to your father's house. You return to the beginning.

Around two thousand years ago, there was a new beginning, when Christ Jesus through His death, resurrection, Church, and Her sacraments gave us the path to new life, to break our bonds of slavery to the world, sin, and death. This was the opportunity for all of humanity, created in the image and likeness of God, to return to the Garden of Eden, to the promised land, to the new Jerusalem. In this way, we were all the entitled sons.

Some might blame God for what happened to His children. Some might ask why He did not chase after them and bring them back home immediately. Yet, what if our eternal Father provided for us, despite our choices that were contrary to His will for us? What if He provided a way for our return home? What if He sent us prophets and saints to warn us so that we might be spared the worst costs of our choice? What if our eternal Father is greater than the father of the bitter and entitled sons, and He sent His beloved and only-begotten son after us?

In almost every city in America where Black Americans are doing statistically the worst, there is a historic Black Catholic church right there amid them. Imagine if those Catholic churches evangelized to their communities' traditional Catholic values and offered unique Catholic worship and devotions, rather than something not much different from the Protestant experience. Would not Black Americans rediscover their inheritance? Would not they find and be captured by the same path that captured Saints Toussaint, Lange, DeLille, and Tolton in the same worship that captured them?

We have tried everything else. Why not try Catholic tradition and try those rigid Catholic values? Why not drop the pseudo religions and embrace the one true Church, outside of which there is no salvation? It worked for these future saints whose stories now follow. Why not everyone else? What do we have to lose?

My Life Changed
The Day We Attended
A Traditional Latin Mass

Arlena Brown

My childhood consisted of me and my brothers going to a non-denominational church with our grandmother. We were raised by our parents, but neither one of them attended church or ever took us to church. Catholicism entered my life at the age of eighteen after going through some very tumultuous years as a young teen.

As a native Californian, speaking about Catholicism was kind of "taboo" in my family, especially because we were Black and lived in a predominately Black neighborhood in Altadena, just twenty minutes from Los Angeles. Imagine my family's surprise when I told them that I met a young Black cradle Catholic man from Detroit named Robert and that I was becoming Catholic.

So many things intrigued me about Robert, but especially the way he would light up speaking about the Lord and his faith. He was raised by his great-grandparents, so knowing that he had a special place in his heart for the elderly was something that we had in common. In my own search for God, knowing more about his faith became something that consumed me. Robert would later take me to RCIA classes where my first teachings of the church took place.

It was honestly so easy to fall in love with. The reverence of the Church is what drew me in initially. Spending a year learning about the faith was so eye-opening. Everything that was said about this "taboo" church was explained. But then there was a fork in the road. My parents had been married and divorced twice and by this point, my father was getting married on the same weekend that my initiation into the church was supposed to take place. Going to my priest for advice was something that happened immediately. He told me that if I had to ask if I should attend the wedding or be initiated into the Church, then I was not ready. Even though that was devastating news, it did not stop me from learning about Catholicism.

After moving to Detroit with Robert and getting engaged to him at the age of twenty, I was finally initiated into the Church. It was one of the happiest days of my life. Robert asked me to marry him, and we got married at the same church that I attended RCIA in California four months later in 2009. It was the first (and only) Catholic wedding I've ever attended! My family was so confused but supportive. We had a rose-giving ceremony to The Blessed Mother during our ceremony. We also jumped the broom, which is an African American tradition, signifying "jumping" into a new life as a married couple. We quickly settled into our lives together and we became pregnant three weeks after the wedding.

At this time, we had no idea of the trials and tribulations our marriage was about to encounter. The amount of stress and anguish that came from being pregnant after just getting married was something that would become a cross of ours together. We also had crosses to bear individually. Robert's great-grandparents were both very ill and all my family lived in California. I had never been away from home at this point more than 20 miles or so and never longer than a week at a time. Just a few weeks after the wedding, my twenty-one-year-old best friend and bridesmaid died suddenly.

Robert was looking for a job in a very turbulent economic society. I battled with a difficult pregnancy and depression. The pressure of marriage began to cave in on us. All the while, we kept attending Mass at his predominately Black home parish faithfully every Sunday. Our wonderful son was born on a cold winter day in 2010. During the spring of both 2011 and 2012, we had two more children, two beautiful daughters.

While I attended school to receive my Bachelor's, we both had jobs, but we knew we wanted to leave Detroit in search of a better life for our growing families. We had been prayerfully discerning where we should live for years. Both of Robert's great-grandparents passed away within two weeks of each other. My maternal grandfather died as well as my paternal grandmother and a host of other friends and family members, whose funeral I was not able to attend. Things seemed dreary at times.

In the spring of 2014, we finally heard God's call and stepped out on faith and moved to Texas. We were nervous and excited. We continued to attend Mass and tried very hard to work on our faith together as a unit as well as individuals while rearing three little children who were two, three, and four at the time. Our faith was continuously tested; however, this was not something that we communicated to each other.

Through the years, we moved many times within the state of Texas. Fort Worth, Dallas, and Tyler in East Texas. We also had a short stint in Fort Collins, Colorado where there were virtually no Black people, let alone Black families. It was during this time that we got our first taste of Latin Mass as well as the Byzantine Rite. We were amazed and a bit intimidated! We would later realize that this experience sowed the seed of Traditional Latin Mass in us.

No matter where we lived, we always made it a point to find a good parish to belong to, even though nothing had compared to our experience in Detroit, where there were actual Black Catholic churches. Even though this was our reality, we never once felt out of place for oftentimes being the only Black family in the entire parish. We were always welcomed, and we made friends with other families easily. People seemed to gravitate towards us and our children.

After we left Colorado, we returned to Texas, but this time we moved to Austin, where an employment opportunity was presented to me. This was the time that we also found ourselves in a homeless shelter until we found an apartment. I worked in the daytime and Robert worked at night. Our children attended a free summer camp so we could work. Our then family of five lived in one room with each other for almost three months. We had to use a community bathroom and we often ate in the shelter's cafeteria. We were stressed and we wondered what our future would look like, but we were happy because we were not worried or afraid.

We started to attend Mass at Saint Mary's Cathedral here in downtown Austin and we loved it. We later moved to a different part of Austin when we found an apartment. We thought we were finally getting a "grip" on life. Our children started to attend Religious Education classes and we attended Mass just a few miles from our new apartment. Our children attended the top school in the area and we both got better jobs. It was like a dream; like we would finally be able to make it. But underneath the surface, both Robert and I were suffering spiritually, but we still never communicated this to each other. Robert traveled often for work, and it left me a bit strained and feeling overwhelmed and unappreciated. We argued a lot. There were times that I felt our marriage would not survive.

Meanwhile, Robert began to attend Latin Mass during his travels. This happened partially because of things he would read and partially because sometimes that was the only Mass he could find in between working and traveling. He would often come back saying how great it was and to be honest, it annoyed me! Trying to understand Latin amid our chaotic lives seemed like such a big obstacle to our religious and spiritual life, especially with the kids being in Religious Education classes.

When we went to Mass in the Novus Ordo Rite, Robert began to change. He seemed to become disconnected from what was happening during Mass. It made me angry. I felt at the time that he was not being a good example to our impressionable children. He asked me so many times to attend Latin Mass, but he was met with a lot of resistance! It wasn't until we attended the symposium of Blessed Carl in Dallas that I began to open my heart to the Traditional Latin Mass and all that it had to offer.

We attended Mater Dai Traditional Latin Mass parish while we were in Dallas and my life was completely changed. Up until that point, I had never seen so many people lined up for confession during Mass. My Confessor spoke to me about my sins, gave me a very tangible and reasonable penance, and he prayed over me in Latin. That changed me forever.

Things seemed like a dream again. It was nice to be on the same page with my husband whom I loved dearly.

Even though we did not know any other Black couples personally that attended Latin Mass, that was not the most important thing to us, although we would have loved to meet some couples like us one day. Usually, when we met Black people in the Church, they either attended Novus Ordo, they were single, they were African, or they were a mixed-race couple.

We later had a great Christmas, attending the earliest Mass we could so that we could spend time together as a family, opening gifts and eating great food. The New Year came and went. In February, we found out we were expecting our fourth child. We were so excited. The children and I were out of school and work for spring break in March of 2020, never thinking that we would never return.

At that time, we experienced what we all know now as the covid-19 shutdowns. My job told me to stay home until they could figure out what was going on. In April, Robert's job told him the same. This happened over the next few months and we both soon realized that we had lost our jobs. Our children were participating in virtual learning for the foreseeable future. The next thing to happen was that our Church closed. We never thought that would happen either, but we took it in stride. We prayed the Rosary between four and five times a week, we prayed the Saint Michael Chaplet and we also "attended" Mass via television. We made it a point to dress as we normally would for Mass. Robert and the children would still kneel during times of kneeling while I would sit as my belly began to grow.

The future that we thought was blossoming in front of us became uncertain. As my pregnancy progressed, we were also unsure of what it would be like to give birth in the hospital since they had many covid restrictions. We had no idea what we would do with our kids during labor. We virtually had no family in our area, just a couple of aunts and a cousin. My doctor told me that taking progesterone shots every week would help me from going into early labor, which is what had been the norm for me with our first three children.

On my way to the doctor's office one day, I began to pray as I was driving about having a home birth. Almost immediately after finishing my prayer, I saw a bumper sticker that read "looking for a doula?" I put the information in my phone as I made a left turn and called the number after my doctor's appointment. This was without a doubt a direct sign from God! At the time, we had no idea what the cost was for midwifery or doula services. God intervened once again, and we found a midwife that would cover the cost of our home birth and a midwife in training that provided us with home birth supplies and a doula.

Their mission was to help Black women have their babies at home because so many Black women are not listened to during birth at the hospital and unfortunately, a lot of Black women end up dying in the hospital because of this during birth. We were so grateful! The only thing that needed to happen was that I had to make it to thirty-seven weeks gestation to have a legal home birth in Texas, which had never happened for me with our first three children. Immediately, we petitioned our church family for prayers. Not only did they pray for us, but they gave us advice on how to keep the baby in as long as possible. They supported me throughout my pregnancy, and we knew it was not because of the color of our skin; they did this because we were brothers and sisters in Christ.

I continued to go to my weekly appointments. There were signs that early labor was a possibility at thirty-two-week gestation, so my doctor ordered me to be on bedrest. During this time, we all continued to pray together, my children helped me with tasks around the house and with getting ready for the baby and Robert did everything he could so that I did not have to get out of bed very much. He truly had a supernatural grace that I had never experienced before. God was truly working through him. Also, during this time, we decided to homeschool our children.

Everything was going so well and at thirty-eight weeks exactly, my water broke at 5:25 am on a Sunday. Our sweet baby girl arrived in this world at 6:39 am. During my whole pregnancy, we prayed to deliver a full-term baby at thirty-seven weeks as well as to have a fast and easy, labor and God granted us both! We couldn't be happier. Meanwhile, we continued to homeschool the kids and Robert had started school to study Cyber Security. We made it a ritual every morning to pray for the intercession of Saint Elizabeth Ann Seton (the Patron Saint of our homeschooling curriculum) and Saint Thomas Aquinas. We said the Texas Pledge and the Pledge of Allegiance.

Our friends from Church set up a meal train for us and brought meals every day to our house and made Doordash donations to us. We felt so blessed and fortunate to be able to have friends that truly cared about our family. Our church soon opened up again. Our baby girl was the first baby in our family to be Baptized in the Latin Rite. It was so beautiful! Our older children received their First Holy Communion in December right before Christmas.

Christ stayed the center of our lives at all times, regardless of the circumstances, hardships, and uncertainty. Going to Latin Mass is the only thing that kept us sane and hopeful through such a trying and chaotic time. Our children did very well in their first year of homeschooling. We later were approached by Associated Press and Fox News to tell about our experience as a Black family that attends Latin Mass and that homeschools their children. By the grace of God, we have been able to stick to our traditions and values.

I Found My Identity In the Catholic Mass

Eric Phillips

"And you shall love the Lord your God with all your heart and with all your soul and with all your mind and with all your strength.... 'You shall love your neighbor as yourself.'"
(MK 12:30)

It is always good to have a good beginning to anything and there is nothing greater than God's goodness. Whoever takes the time to read this I am surely grateful. Most importantly, may all, in some way be inspired to further God's kingdom after reading this.

My parents Baptized me as a Catholic as an infant and I was later enrolled in a Catholic grammar school which I attended for eight years. After I completed grammar school, I went on to enroll in a Catholic High School. Yet, from my earliest days on this Earth

up through high school, the word, "Catholic" had no uniqueness to it whatsoever. It was just a label, nothing more.

Why was this my understanding? As with most things, it starts in the home. When parents don't understand the faith, the children will likely follow in misunderstanding.

In order to honor my mother and father yet be truthful in this brief explanation of my faith journey, I will say that generations of Catholics have been betrayed by some Catholic educators in so much that the faith has not been taught, apologetics has been abandoned, the image of the Church has been misconfigured so that its identity is simply a social institution that makes one feel good about what one wants whenever one wants it. It has become the "Have it Your Way Church". So, my parents were not properly formed in the Faith and thus, could not teach me the basics of it.

Yet, it was made known to me by them that God most certainly does exist and there are consequences for behaviors.

My grandfather was instrumental in teaching me about the different stories in Scripture of how God, time and time again, saved His people and how God, time and time again, reprimanded His people. And I am most eternally grateful for the Baptism that my parents provided for me.

In hindsight, my school was not a source of solid formation either. In my ignorance of the Faith, I did much and held an attitude that was unbecoming of a Catholic. I was certain that God existed and that He should be feared but I did not know that He left one Church. Yet, God placed something in me from the time I could remember that would inevitably lead me into the light of His Church.

I had always loved history, philosophy, and critical thinking. I simply have joy in discovering the many depths of a concept. I would think about concepts and their implications for everyday life. I would be more than happy to debate my thoughts with others as I found much joy in debating as well. I considered myself a Christian apologetic because it was so much fun to me explaining God's presence even though He is corporally invisible, a natural joy.

In my time as a pre-teen, a teen, and into my early 20s I just didn't know I had already been baptized into the Faith that provided me with all the tools necessary to build on this joy. I hadn't known what I already had. This truth stings but I am grateful for the Lord showing me the heritage to which I belong.

It was my pursuit to unravel the mysteries of the Old Testament that set a beautiful trap for my heart that had me fully embrace all the infallible teachings of the Catholic Faith. I knew that many attacks against Christianity came from misunderstandings of the Old Testament. So, I proceeded to find every contentious

Old Testament passage, identify the possible criticism, and provide a response. I would read the passages and look for commentary on them. Protestant theologians such as Ravi Zacharias and Dr. William Lane Craig gave very informative talks. Yet, there was one passage in Scripture that, no matter how hard I tried, I never found sensible commentary on it. The passage was Psalms 137 v. 8-9, "O daughter of Babylon, doomed to be destroyed, blessed shall he be who repays you with what you have done to us! Blessed shall he be who takes your little ones and dashes them against the rock." I read this and could not see a way this could be explained other than the plain meaning. No matter the commentary I looked at, nothing spoke to me as making sense.

Why would a 'loving God' bless those that would kill children? How would I respond to an atheist's challenge? This was a stumbling block for me until I listened to a talk by the then Fr. Barron. Unbeknownst to me before I listened, he made a brief reference to this passage of Scripture that became the key to so much more. He explained that a man by the name of "Origen" explained the verse like this. The little ones of Babylon are the evil thoughts and desires that harbor in one's mind and heart. We are to take them and bash them against the Rock who is Christ.

I had never heard an interpretation of something seemingly so violent but so beautifully connected to who Christ is. I had to know who this Origen was. The name sounded weird, but the interpretation invigorated me. I studied Origen and found he was a prolific early Church theologian. I read many of his writings and was left amazed at his level of interpretation and how he would take so many passages of the Old Testament and interpreted how they foreshadowed the New. To me, he was the best I ever encountered and what was more astounding was that he lived approximately 1800 years ago and still gave greater insights on Scripture than those of today. And I asked myself, "Was it just him in his time that had this ability, or were there others too?" It was one of the most crucial questions I ever asked myself as it led me into the beauty of the Catholic Faith.

From Origen to Polycarp onto St. Justin Martyr to St. Cyprian and so on I discovered them all by God's grace and my soul was energized by their wit, intelligence, understanding, witness, and most importantly, their love of God which oozes out between the words of their writings. I was truly humbled by them as I formerly told myself that there was no way someone so ancient could be wiser than someone in modern times. This is a disposition I am afraid too many holds today. Yet, the Lord showed me my pride and showed me how wrong I had been.

I read the clearest and sensible understandings of Scripture I had ever read by reading the Early Church Fathers. They did it with seemingly so much ease. And I knew through my study of history that many of them did their elaborations of Scripture and Church teaching while under murderous persecutions. Yet, this reality did not stop them. They continued to teach and preach against sin, gaining supernatural faith, the power of the Sacraments, what it means to love God, etc.

Before I found the Catechism, I found the Early Church Fathers. They communicated as they spoke to God every day about every question on their mind and every question they had ever been asked. I was truly enamored by their writings. It is disappointing to me I had not known them earlier but that is a discussion for a different time. Inspired and humbled by their witness I learned to let go of pride and submit to every infallible teaching of the Church. This has helped me find a peace I previously had not known existed. It is truly a peace not of this world, and it has birthed a child-like joy in me. I am always amazed at not only what God has done for me but the clarity of what He desires of us communicated through the Church despite the vain attempts throughout the ages to simply doubt the Church and Her authority given by Christ.

There is a real split in the Church today. To me, the problem is a very feint understanding of what the Church is, why it is needed, and a complete rejection of the devil's very active involvement to severely harm the Church through several vices. The rejection of Satan's activity comes from, in my opinion, the rejection of Hell being a real place, the false notion that all or most people go to Heaven, the convenient forgetfulness that our Lord is the God of love as well as the God of justice or some combination of these misguided understandings.

There is no fear of God and because of this, we have become fertile ground for vices. And these vices, have made us their home, have made us comfortable with spiritual slothfulness, and have removed the oxygen so that no fire for the Faith can be lit. Yet, the power of vice is such because we have not even glanced at virtue. So, we should aspire to glance at virtue so we can meet our other friend called humility.

Humility makes it so much easier to say what many refuse to say, to believe. The Catholic Church is right in all of Her doctrines and dogma and all of humanity can only benefit from it. The word "all" can't be substituted for "some". This is not the easiest thing to admit to oneself but there is real pleasure and peace once it is embraced in mind and heart. One just needs to let go of the personal pride that says, "no, the Church can't be that", "the crimes of the Church are many, how can anyone say their doctrines are infallible?" "I feel this teaching or that teaching is insensitive so this can't be true." All these utterances need to be put on mute, even for just a moment, and we should just pray, "Lord give me the humility to believe in You and Your Body for my sake, for the sake of my family and the whole world." I believe earnestly praying this, in all sincerity, will help one eagerly accept the Catholic

Church as having the charism of infallibility when teaching on faith and morals as described in the Catechism.

For me, and I think for most Black Catholics in regions that were colonized by the European powers of the 15th to the 19th centuries, there is a stigma of the Catholic faith unique to our historical cultural experience. The stigma is that the faith is the European faith that requires its tenants to view the heroes of the faith as being "white" and the saviors of the world. This stigma, I too, struggled with before placing my full trust and confidence in the Church.

It was discouraging to me that throughout my time growing up nearly all the images I saw of Catholics were White. Knowing world history and geography I knew where Africa was located and where the Middle East was located and I knew that even if one goes back 2000 years, those areas were not populated by people who we would call "White" today so, why would a Church that is purportedly trustworthy constantly depict saints from those regions as white? From the Old Testament to the New Testament, all white? Why the inaccuracy? These questions were my great barrier to fully embracing the faith. And it was the Early Church Fathers again that helped me in this. A good number of them, being from N. Africa and the Middle East and loving the faith so much understood the mission given to them by Christ to take the faith into the whole world.

The Church from its origin had always been a multi-colored face and that's just the truth. It was the early Christians who looked to these Early Church Fathers and teachers: St. Augustine, St. Cyprian, St. Anthony of Egypt, St Athanasius, St. Monica, Sts. Felicity and Perpetua, St. Clement of Alexandria, etc… for guidance, instruction, and inspiration. This instruction went from Africa and the Middle East into the rest of the world. The mantle was then passed onto Europe and, it seems to me, now the mantle is being passed back to Africa but this time it is reaching the whole span of the continent.

Knowing the origin of these Church Fathers and the historical transmission of the faith disarmed me of my apprehension of the white imagery. It no longer was a barrier to my faith. I think we, as Catholics who are Black, should harness our creative abilities and fill our churches and religious literature with diverse images of the saints, of the Lord and Blessed Mother.

I am sure I am not the only one who has struggled with that apprehension. It is one thing to say the color of the images does not matter when the majority of the images are already palatable to how one has traditionally thought of their appearance but to say this to a people whose existing historical narrative within certain countries has been marked by chattel slavery and constant social struggle to have the same rights as their fellow citizens are apathetic.

The color of the saints matter as this, apart from being historically accurate, provides a visually compelling statement for the present and ancient reality that Black boys and girls can be, have been and will be saints too. Color is an issue because, we, as a society, have made it one and the best way to address the issue is to understand every Catholic has the right to see the face of the Church that Peter saw at Pentecost. Yet, with every right comes a duty.

Every Catholic has the duty to evangelize like Peter and Paul and, by this, we will see the multi-colored face of the Church Militant. To be clear, salvation is about the Sacraments and not skin color but getting people to the Sacraments is aided by acknowledging that the physical body does play a part in one's identity. In that identity we hope to see dignity, appreciating one's skin color helps build this dignity.

There is no greater place than the Mass to find our true identity in Christ. Simply because the Eucharist is offered to all those properly disposed to receive it. Everyone, regardless of who you are, what you have done, or what you look like, everyone is offered the same Body and Blood of Jesus Christ. The God of the universe wants to be inside of us even in the literal sense. Yet, we must cleanse our temple in preparation for His reception. This is done through Baptism and Confession. Let us appreciate the miracles God works on a daily basis, particularly at Mass, then let us look forward to the miracles that are to come.

Related to this discussion regarding our identity and the Mass is the aesthetics, language, and everything else involved in the presentation of the liturgy, most particularly the Roman Rite. Should one always kneel and have the Eucharist placed on the tongue? Are drums and guitars allowed for music? Should the priest face ad orientem for most of the duration of the Mass? These are but some of the questions which are concomitant with the debate regarding the liturgy within the Catholic world. It is a debate that I have not taken a strong position on either way as I have not done many studies into pre-Vatican II and Vatican II itself. I, am most familiar with the "Novus Ordo". I do believe the word "reverence" has subjective, relative understandings of what "reverence" looks like and to whom. Yet, Sacred Scripture and Sacred Tradition do lay down some blueprint regarding what reverence is, so it is not completely a subjective thing.

Considering the debates this diversity of liturgy has triggered I think it is the laity whose attendance or lack thereof at Mass will show what liturgy the Holy Spirit is most honored by. For the Holy Spirit only enjoys what is holy and why should anyone seek to reject or restrict what is holy? Unlike, abortion, euthanasia, and the contortion of marriage away from the biblical understanding that it is a covenant of one man one woman united by God, these all have Catholic teachings that demand the utmost immediate attention that we must fight head-on but when it comes to the controversy regarding the "Novus Ordo" vs "Traditional Latin Rite" (and any other similar debate) I don't think a head-on approach is needed by either side of the debate to conclude what form/rite of the liturgy we need or need more of.

Bishops should provide and allow access to both at reasonable times so that working people have the chance to attend. In my opinion, over time it will become apparent which liturgy has the most attendance, most young people, most families, most frequent tithers, and most people willing to get involved in a parish ministry. In my opinion, and now speaking strictly to the Novus Ordo and Traditional Latin Rite, as one increases in attendance and attention the other, if it does not decrease or dwindle, won't see the same rate of increase in attendance and growth as the other. In my humble opinion, these will be the signs as to where the Holy Spirit finds genuine faith in Him, faith that the Blessed Mother and saints truly do intercede for us, and faith in all the power of all the Sacraments. Wherever the Holy Spirit sees the most faith, the authentic faith, He will provide that community with abundant graces to carry on the worship due to Him. Honest church officials of a good heart, will see this too and will make administrative changes to ensure the liturgy is always readily available to those who thirst for it.

It hurts to see many Catholics who do not see the Eucharist for what it is but, many teachings of the faith simply aren't believed. Some will vainly, privately, or publicly state they need to change because we need to have, what is considered modern understanding. We struggle with understanding the real threat of Satan, Hell, and the realness of the Eucharist. We further struggle with addressing the pre-eminent issue of our day, abortion.

To be clearer, and to call it what it is, by abortion I mean the murder of children. We have adopted a lethargic slothful attitude regarding abortion because we no longer have faith in children because we no longer have faith in mothers and fathers because we no longer have faith in marriage, because we no longer have supernatural faith in God's grace which the evils of this world can't limit. The word "pre-eminence" is not needed to know it is the pre-eminent issue. It is the pre-eminent and cornerstone issue for all else. If not, then every other cause we soldier for is about the utility of a person.

I cannot believe we have entered a time where a rational, theological argument is needed to explain why it is the pre-eminent cornerstone (I'll call this 'foundatience' meaning pre-eminent issue that is foundational to all societal issues) issue. All societal challenges we have lean on justice to ensure people are understood as people not, utilities. If pregnancy and the unborn child do not proverbially scream with acclamation, "Innocence!" and "Hope!" then we won't see with urgency the call for justice when the crime of murder is levied upon them and, If we don't address this call for justice for the most innocent then our fight for the poor, the refugee, the disabled is a flakey, fleeting thing because we have exchanged the fight for the recognition of the imago dei within all people for the fight for the material gain void of evangelistic aspirations. Spiritual poverty is real too.

We have a misplaced faith. The lives of the unborn are equal in intrinsic value to anyone else yet the crime of murder has no equal. So, we should work to save the unborn, help the poor, and help the elderly simultaneously without pitting one cause against the other.

The alleviation of poverty should be pursued as a means (not an end) to potentially aid in evangelization, the raising and nurturing of children, and the promulgation of families. Our faith is not based on compromises like the world of politics but supernatural faith. Yet, there is no societal challenge equal to embracing the intrinsic value inherent in all of us because we are made in God's image and likeness which is present in us from conception to death. We need to be honest with ourselves.

As the number of Black Catholics in the U.S. dwindles (parallel with the decline in many Catholic demographics), as Mass participation decreases, the bishops will find more reason not to listen to our concerns. The same logic can even be applied to our representation in our Democratic Republic, numbers are not the be-all in all, but they do matter, and we haven't been on the upshoot but the downward tick for decades.

How do we solve this? I think firstly we need to realize it's not white supremacy that is the cause of this but something more ancient and much perfidious. It is the spirit of Pharoah that commanded the Hebrew midwives to kill the Hebrew newborns because Pharoah was threatened by the ever-growing number of Hebrew people. Typical of His saving fashion God increased the number of His people and blessed the Midwives with families. God, knowing full well, His people were slaves and had an economic and cultural system fashioned against the prosperity of His people, His response to the Midwives' faithfulness was to increase their number, amid hostility, and this increase in number brought about the saints that the Holy Spirit would work through to liberate His people from bondage, in all its forms.

God's grace works with faith before anything else. Who doesn't know the name of Moses? Who doesn't know the name of Aaron? Who doesn't know the name of Miriam? Who doesn't know the name of Joshua? So, we first need to properly identify where the most serious attack on our community is taking place and not look at this fight mundanely, that is to say, in a purely economic or secular justice sense but to firstly realize we are in a spiritual fight that has been waged since the time of our first parents Adam and Eve. I can only say, with most seriousness, that this spiritual fight is real.

It is apparent to me that our communities have been attacked by efforts to dissolve the family and abort the young. Once realizing the spiritual conflict, we are in the laity can proceed to establish concrete initiatives (with proper healthy debate) that will spur Sacramental marriages. What State and local government initiatives can be instituted to encourage people to marry? Are there any financial/tax incentives? Are there any education incentives? Has space for Catholic family counseling been established and developed? If not, how is that done? How much government involvement is needed in this? Are there any foundations or non-profits we can establish as laity to help spurn marriages? What can we citizens do to ensure the longevity, growth, and safety of the adoption industry? The clergy would have the most important part in this. As providing people with incentives to marry is not enough but reminding the faithful why we have the Sacrament of Matrimony is paramount.

One idea is to have processions with newly wedded couples (presumably sometime after the honeymoon), processing in a prominent position, which starts from the outside of the Church to the inside. Invite married Catholic couples to speak to Catholic school children, together. As mentioned earlier in this essay, providing more images of saints of various backgrounds. Clergy should also take more time addressing the statistics through the decades concerning the decline in Baptisms, Marriages, Attendance, School and Parish closures, and make graphs visible on Parish websites. These are just ideas put forth to spark further thought and conversation about what can be done to encourage people to marry. It is not a comprehensive study. Yet, nothing compares to being that lived example of a Catholic. That, in and of itself, is the evangelistic work needed to turn society's worn, wearied, desperate but spiritually thirsty gaze towards the Sacraments of the Church.

I am well aware of the concern some have expressed regarding the emphasis one may place on protecting the unborn and allegedly not caring about any other stage of life. I normally find two assumptions in that argument that firstly, lacks justice and, secondly, deprives citizens of those debates which are proper and necessary to its domain. In my opinion, it should never follow that one's zealous fight for the unborn produces the assumption in another that such a zealous person has no care for that child's education, upbringing, access to a livable wage, etc. Just because we don't see the certain actions by others when we choose to look is not grounds for concluding that that person places no effort in this or that. "Thou shalt not bear false witness against thy neighbor." This encompasses more than lying but creating a narrative about a person or people based on assumptions and not facts.

If God is to judge us accordingly to how we judged others we need to seriously consider is that the accusation we want to make is against the character of a person or people we don't know? The argument then goes from claiming the apathy within the other and linking this said apathy to said person proving they are apathetic because of policies that the said person is alleged not to support. Without a doubt, we as a Christian people are commissioned to help the poor, the sick, the vulnerable, the widow, and the orphan. Yet, how this is done with or without the help of the government is that discussion that belongs to the domain of constant public debate. Meaning that one may disagree with a said policy and support another, articulate their position, hear opposing arguments, and make the appeal to others as to why their position is the most efficacious; a person should be able to do this without another being accused that a person does not care about another because another's policy isn't supported. The reasons for not supporting a policy may have something to do with the policy itself (and the philosophy behind it) and not any alleged apathy.

This is why these discussions belong to the domain of constant public debate. To try to remove or discourage debate from its proper place/domain disenfranchises concerned citizens (which should and does include Catholics) from being exposed to the existence of multiple potentially propitious ideas and puts one on the precipice of making their own [Type here] Eric Phillips policy one of an infallible nature. Yet, this infallibility belongs only to our Triune God who has expressed Himself through His Body, The Catholic Church. Let us adopt the attitude that policymaking should be our offering to God we hope He accepts.

We can't honor the Sacrament of the Eucharist without honoring the Sacrament of Confession, likewise, we can't do justice to ourselves without first recognizing where the heart of the problem lies. We all have a responsibility in the Church's decline.

The years I spent procrastinating about learning about our Faith, yes, I share responsibility concerning the current state of the Church. When our numbers increase because families are having children and raising them in the faith when our numbers increase because we are evangelizing like the Apostles, our presence in the Church in the U.S. will give us a more ambient voice but that voice should always be wedded to the perennial teachings of the Faith so that the spirit of Pharoah never returns.

The whole Church will benefit as more Black Catholics, Hispanic Catholics, White Catholics, and Asian Catholics will increase the opportunities for cultural engagement amongst themselves. Yet, I don't want to conclude this engagement without mentioning prayer is always the start of everything beautiful. The supremacists and racists amongst us are covert in their operation. They will show themselves as the faithful push for marriages, children, and adoption. And in this push, self-hate will be revealed too. It is my opinion, that racists are less concerned about what I can do as an individual but more concerned about what, I, with a family can do. And no one is more racist than Satan himself. This is why when we pray, we should not only pray for ourselves but that God's peace permeates the entire world and all people. He will hear us, and our yoke will be made light.

It is good to remember that there is no vice virtue can't overcome because virtue is from God. We need to think less in terms of haves and have not and more in terms of vice and virtue. When we, as a people, sleep with virtue, eat with virtue, work with virtue, breathe in virtue, when we no longer regard it as an ethereal concept for human existence, when it becomes the foremost thought within us, we will be where God has destined for us to be and our whole Church and country will only benefit from it

"If my people who are called by my name humble themselves and pray and seek my face and turn from their wicked ways, then I will hear from heaven and will forgive their sin and heal their land."
(2 Chronicles 7:14)

My First Black Catholic Priest

Géraldine Précil

Blackness: What It Is, and What It Ain't
Skin. It covers every visible part of our person. The visibility of Black skin is singular. Black skin cloaks one's humanity and evokes associations.

Black skin is warm: when I was a public sinner, men told me that it feels like velvet. When Black skin blushes, it doesn't redden, but it shines. When not oiled, it becomes ashen; with oil, it glistens, and it is notoriously wrinkle-free: African countenances don't crack. But not all Black people have Black skin, so hue is not our common denominator. Neither is hair, IQ, geographic location, language, rhythm, temperament, or religion…

Blackness is not defined or lived in opposition to whiteness, save in the racially obsessed. Blackness is not a death sentence, nor is it a life sentence – it is lived more like a marriage than having the soul-rending finality of a funeral. It is not purgation or a curse, or an immutable destiny. It is not a defining characteristic of my personality or my culture. In itself, it does not create community or alienation, and it is not a deviation from a norm. It probably doesn't inspire or condemn. Blackness has no inherent meaning other than what is ascribed to it, but malefactors on the left and right do ascribe meaning.

What Blackness Can Be is a Complication
Its apprehension can be a barrier or a nonverbal conversation. Blackness can render a person into an avatar, or a representation of a private and invisible self that is denied or hidden, only to be accused and exonerated in the court of the confessional or condemned in the interior monologue that I hear in my own voice just as I believe Satan's voice was heard within Eve, as her own. One Black person can become all Black people – a prototypical humanity. The Black man is a symbolic composite of typical impulses and drives, a soul, and a spirit fused into a being lower than angels but above beasts. To be Black is to inhabit a persona, enclosed in the skin, and bound to the world as though by an umbilical cord, or to be tied to a pillar. To be Black is too long for the transcendent and the desire to live beyond the tangible and material, including the cloak of skin or sin, but it is also to fear the ends of both sin and skin. I did not know it, because they were all White men, but Father D. and the other priests of the Latin Mass fraternity were Black.

Dogma
In 2018, I was diagnosed with a rare and aggressive cancer. I was told that the cancer has a high risk of recurrence, and that recurrence is often rapidly fatal. I joined a support group. Before joining, I thought to myself, "If this cancer is aggressive and if it has a high risk of recurrence, won't there be a number of deaths?" I didn't want to answer my own question. I clicked, "Join Group." I got my answer.

Women died every week. They were White, Arab, Latina, and Black. Some women were in their seventies, while others were in their forties or thirties; the youngest was in her twenties, and she left behind four young children. She had been diagnosed with an early-stage disease, like me. They were thin, fit or heavy, poor or upper class. Some thought they were having migraines, only to be told that it had spread to their brain and that they had one and a half years to live. Some were told that they had weeks… I started to understand why they called this cancer the "wild card" of the breast cancer world. It started to feel as though Amon Leopold Göth had stepped out of "Schindler's List" and he was shooting us at random from his balcony; I could feel gunmetal against my temple.

Modernism, the synthesis of all heresies, is the deification of the carnal man's intellect and it is the usurpation of God. Modernism is self-worship. In this materialist religion that accepts physical reality as the culmination of man's being and purpose, death is anathema. It's banished to the peripheries of experience and there is no psychological template with which to integrate death. It's condemned as an unnatural intruder. This stance is cruel and deluded, for many of the women did not know that they were actually dying.

Modern medicine can keep people working and functioning until mere days before death. We were pumped full of steroids, and many felt invincible. Antiemetics were crossed with sedatives. Most were taking opiates, and some must have taken something harder. A few were drinking during chemo. Women who were given a year to live spent their days posting on the support group and surfing the internet. Others had "ego disintegration." In short, they went mad, and they were institutionalized.

But cancer treatment didn't have the effect on me that one would think, because of what I had finally accepted as the truth, the day I was diagnosed.

The doctor and a nurse came into the examination room. They weren't laughing at my jokes and there was a suffocating silence in the room. I stopped smiling. I knew that I had the rare cancer that they had warned me about: I was too young, and I was fit; I'd even lost one hundred pounds eating an organic diet. I am Black. The lifestyle factors didn't add up to risk factors for any ordinary breast cancer diagnosis, and my genetics pointed to an unusual one. But it wasn't just a logical assessment.

Something in me started to… pulsate. It was like anticipating a full-body sneeze. There was a physical crescendo, like Beethoven's ninth symphony. I wasn't listening to the doctor.

"Are you okay, honey? Do you want me to call someone?"

I put up my hand to shush her. She and the nurse glanced at one another, discreetly. It was a whisper: "Credo in unum Deum, Patrem omnipotentem, (I believe in one God, the Father Almighty) factorem cæli et terræ, visibilium omnium et invisibilium (maker of heaven and earth, of all things visible and invisible)." I heard it again, louder. And again.

Like most Catholics who came of age in the post-conciliar era, I didn't have catechesis: I had coercive persuasion. They raped our minds. Modernism is actually moral nihilism. I was taught, albeit implicitly, that faith is subjective, as is truth – therefore, truth cannot exist. To the modernist, monotheism oppressively renders other "faiths" illegitimate and orthodox Catholicism is "triumphalist" (although one wonders how other "faiths" could have legitimacy or illegitimacy if truth is subjective?). The universe was a random event, so there is no creative intelligence that designed it; the only reality is the visible one…

I couldn't get through the creed, so I had stopped singing it, just as I stopped believing in the Real Presence, so I stopped receiving Communion. The momentum of my incredulity built, and I stopped attending Mass altogether. I wanted to self-identify as an "ex-Catholic," but there was a problem: Catholicism was fused to my genetics and culture. It was the only mental map I could use to navigate reality and that didn't disintegrate when confronted with new data. I couldn't shake it. And now there was a formidable void confronting me: the potential end of my selfhood. Something within me settled and yielded. Inside myself, I said, "Yes, credo…" I wiped my tears and told the doctor that I wanted immediate and aggressive treatment. Within two weeks, I was having chemo designed for women with end-stage cancer.

And I followed this interruptive consciousness, the pulsation within myself that led me into the Presence of God and out of my own psyche, during chemo, surgeries, and being confined to my bed; or being quarantined in my home or collapsing in the middle of the night, or being placed in an isolation ward – but these things happened far less frequently to me than the other women.

At the beginning of treatment, my doctor told me that my immune system would collapse by week eight. We'd figure out what we'd do then, he said. For the other women, a collapsed immune system meant the temporary or permanent cessation of chemo and the likely spread of the cancer. Week eight was branded in my psyche.

On week eight, I signed into the treatment ward. The phlebotomist drew my blood. In the waiting room, I steeled myself to be told I'd be going home and that treatment would be postponed. But strangely, I felt really good. The nurse was holding my lab results. She was flummoxed.

"Well, your lab results are perfect."

They really were. We both stared at them. My immune system didn't collapse until five more weeks.

My hair took months to fall out. I was up at my usual 4:00 a.m to pray before going to work at an alternative education center in the inner city. While undergoing oral chemotherapy, three days after being released from a Floridian hospital after my immune system collapsed, I did the stations of the cross on a mountaintop in South America on a Fulbright Fellowship. I had only partial use of my hands and feet, and I had a cane – and I'm terrified of heights. I wore a scapular and a miraculous medal. Throughout treatment, I rarely wept, but I wasn't in denial or numb; when I did weep, it was often for the mothers in our support group who were leaving their babies. I wept when my friends died, and once, I was the last person to speak to a beloved friend while he was lucid, reading his favorite verse, Philippians 4:13: "I can do all this through Him who gives me strength." Another friend texted me to pray for her death because she couldn't bring herself to do it. I told her that she was beloved by God, and asked God to take her between sobs. I never heard from my friend again. I would text her that she was beloved by God over and over again, or I would call her phone just to hear her voice, but I had to stop. It hurt. She had died hard.

When asked why I wasn't suffering, I said it was the steroids, but I knew it was Someone else, Someone at the center of our being, and of all being. God incarnated as an antidote to alienation, the curse of our expulsion from paradise. Someone else must live within us, if we're to live with God: we are tabernacles of flesh. Catholics have a portable God.

The creed wasn't just a crescendo in my mind: it was the whole symphony. I now accepted dogma as the crystallization of truth, like an insect frozen in amber, only the insect was alive.

God hadn't pulled the trigger.

White Box Theater
It's February 2020. My doctors label me as having "no evidence of disease." With this type of cancer, doctors are reluctant to declare one cured or in remission, because of its unpredictability. I've known women who went from "no evidence of disease," to stage four within four months. It doesn't matter anymore. I surrender to the reality that the past is a canceled check and that tomorrow never comes.

But there's fallout. I have tinnitus and I've lost some hearing. My vision has changed. I have neuropathy in my hands and feet, and I sometimes use a cane or a walker — I'm in my forties. There's also nerve damage to my central nervous system: my body has difficulty regulating my temperature and heart rate. If I'd had any more chemo, this condition may have become life-threatening. There's arthritis in all my joints and my teeth are rotting. I have a mild cognitive impairment and memory loss (the memory loss isn't an entirely bad thing; I've forgotten many traumas and resentments). It takes me three hours to get ready for work in the morning, because I move so slowly -- now, I'm up at 3:00 am to pray before work. My physical frailty has impacted my spiritual practice and stamina. I had accepted the first sentence of the creed. Why not accept the second sentence, Christ in the Blessed Sacrament, if hagiographies and tradition purport its healing power? There weren't any other options.

But there was a problem: the only priestly fraternity that offers the Latin Mass in my town is deemed "canonically irregular."

People spoke vehemently of the society. They were accused of White supremacy and there was allegedly a vocally antisemitic cleric formerly of their ranks. Others labeled them as fanatics. My Haitian mulatta grandmother was a "Lefebvrist," and her Catholic convent school-inflected, bona fide Catholic asceticism was alarming: my grandmother slept with a wooden board under her mattress, a crucifix under her pillow, and a rosary wrapped around her wrist like Padre Pio; she was an auto-flagellant. She quite literally prayed in her sleep, as had her own mother before her, and her grandmother. My highfalutin university education taught me that my impoverished and docile grandmother was a grandiose masochist (even though she was desperately praying for me). I'd been attending the Tridentine mass off-and-on for nearly twenty years, but I was ambivalent. I knew its spiritual and symbolic potency. I understood its profound significance as a synthesis of Western civilization's Christian ideals. I even accepted the miraculous and - irrespective of the faults of parishioners and clerics- I never doubted the implacability of their belief. But I was a lover of the world, and I wanted my freedom. I didn't know that Aquinas said that true freedom is the freedom to choose between a diversity of good. I still chose the wrong or corrupt.

But hadn't people said the very same things about me once they'd learned I attended an Indult mass? Was there any truth to the slurs they made about me? Had anyone ever satisfactorily explained to me which part of myself I sought to oppress or annihilate by attending a religious service: the White, Black, or Native parts? I decided to return to Mass.

The mission chapel was surprisingly minimalist. It reminded me of a black box theater, but mostly white (pun intended). It was a Spanish-style mission. Jeanne D'arc was at the entrance (one of my grandmother's favorite saints!). There were small stations of the cross plaques accented with a Wedgewood-esque blue. I saw the Infant Jesus of Prague, Our Lady of Good Success, and a painting of Saint Thomas Moore. I stopped in my tracks. I'm very devoted to Saint John Fisher, his contemporary who was also martyred over Henry the VIII's divorce petition. There was something imposing about the tabernacle and altar. There was a formidable presence about it. During the Mass, it was as though an entity presided over the Mass, the priest, and the people.

The priest was young and blonde, and his sermon stunned me: it was the first time I had ever heard a sermon about a miraculous conversion attributed to the miraculous medal, to which I'm devoted. I love having a bit of the supernatural on my person at all times. And he'd actually said the word "virtue" more than once! They spoke my language. I knew I'd be back, but I was too frail to make the trek. I had to watch the Mass on YouTube. I had no idea that Mass was not the only thing I'd see on an electronic screen, or that my isolation would be prolonged for yet another year...

Some of the kids at school were sick with a weird flu. The next month, our school was shut down. The week before Easter Sunday, I developed gastrointestinal symptoms and then the dreaded fever. I asked my aged parents to stay away from me as I isolated myself within their house. I prayed just like my grandmother.

On Easter Sunday, I asked myself why I didn't just pick up my mat and walk. I did just that. The fever had broken. I watched the Mass on the internet. They were outdoors.

I realized that praying without ceasing wasn't evidence of neurosis. Quite to the contrary, I was becoming remarkably non-neurotic. My doctors and the nurses kept asking why I was so calm, and why I was always smiling. I was too timid to respond, but I decided to turn this quarantine into a religious retreat for however long it lasted. I was well enough to return to Mass over the summer.

But there was a problem, so far as I had conceived of it: I had seen the race riots. I was astounded by the racial rhetoric I was encountering and the resurgence of cultural Marxism in the openly Marxist Black Lives Matter organization. I was appalled, but I was also concerned about the implications for Black people who were unaffiliated or who were opposed to cultural Marxism, like myself; my racial and ethnic ambiguity as a mixed-race Haitian didn't help. If the fraternity had a reputation for White supremacy and extremism, what might I encounter? I decided that like the support groups, life would provide the answer.

Ligature

(Enter dramatis personae.)
I have returned to Mass. I'm uninvolved with peoples' reactions to me at work, in the outside world, in my own family, or church.

People are not themselves these days, so I divest. As we say in twelve-step fellowships, my aim is to remain in a fit spiritual condition. We also say that people don't do anything to you, but they do and say things for themselves. I want Communion with God in lieu of a pathological community.

I attend the early Mass, but I stay to pray and meditate. A priest enters from the sacristy, at stage right. It's Father D. He gives a catechism class before the Mass. There is something distinct about him that doesn't translate in the online videos.

The sign of the cross is my favorite prayer. It's an invocation and a profession of faith, and hurrying it mindlessly seems akin to taking the name of the Lord in vain. He kneels before the tabernacle and crosses himself slowly. And then Father D. closes his eyes. He opens them, and then he stares at the tabernacle as though he's looking into someone's eyes. He exhales slowly. His chest heaves and expands and then settles. His eyes are fixed on the tabernacle. He begins to pray slowly, and with intention, whispering. What Father D. has is something that I've only found at the Tridentine Mass and other Eastern liturgies: reverential intimacy. Father D. seems to enter the tabernacle of his own heart. In Ebonics, we'd say that "He not playin'!" But I don't perceive malice or coercive intent in his person. His aura is placid and there's the glimmer of something else… sorrow?

I'm curious. I watch his every gesture. I remember the etymology of the word, "religion." In Latin, religare means to bind. A priest once told me that the term has a more emphatic meaning, as in to fuse or to weave together, like a wound that is healing. The aim of the Catholic is to fuse himself with God.

A priest in a black cassock has a formidable presence. I've heard Protestants and hostile Catholics denigrate cassock-wearing priests as grim reapers or phantoms. For abuse survivors, a cassock is an intense trigger. But for a traditionalist Catholic, priests seem like black angels, bearing messages and persevering through missions as conduits for God's grace: if grace were water and the congregation was dying of thirst, the priest is a Roman aqueduct. They stand beyond and above the flock, quite literally, at the pulpit. The danger is that we relate to the idealized symbol of the priesthood rather than to Christ himself. Or conversely, we become fixated on the clergy, and we abandon one another, whom we supernaturally adopt as a family of choice in mutual intercession. If the priest's persona is smashed, his authority evaporates, as do the weakly binding ties of the Catholic community. That's why a priest should not simply assume a public persona. Ideally, a priest should be the bearer of a radiantly transformed heart.

Father D.'s homilies are elegant. Typically, traditionalist priests have sermons that are restrained and pragmatic. The topics are not frivolous, but the homily places a distant second behind the Mass. Father D.'s sermons have the requisite restraint and pragmatism as he undoes the knots of nonexistent or atrocious post-conciliar religious education. But he relates Catholic principles and practice to lived experiences. Common topics include the causes and the heart of suffering and wounding, and the antidote: God's grace -- but they're not condescending or condemnatory. I wonder how he knows? It seems that Father D. is not just a priest but a man, and a human. He is of the earth.

But I'll eventually learn my role in the drama, and how I relate to Father D...

My prayer life is intensifying. My whole life is becoming a prayer. I wake up at 3:00 am to pray for others. I'm praying the Little Office. I'm praying the rosary. I add the Seven Sorrows Chaplet during my lunch break. I say the Publican's Prayer throughout the day. I'm reading the Lives of the Saints. Act Of Contrition. Saint Patrick's Breastplate. A perpetual Miraculous Medal Novena and consecration... I understand Aquinas, a veritable miracle! This isn't tiring or obsessive. It's actually calming. But these aren't the most shocking changes...

Something is happening to me during Mass. I'm having difficulty following along in the missal. There's a strange mist obscuring my vision. So, I pray the Mass. After I leave Mass, I start to realize that it doesn't seem that anyone had been there, save the priest and the small children. I wouldn't be able to identify anyone else in a police lineup. And then there's an astonishing change.

At Mass, I get plunged into darkness and I can only meditate upon one thing, sometimes for hours, like Christ's wounds, or droplets of sweat dripping from Christ's face or the Crown Of Thorns, or the Annunciation. Conversely, I can also follow the Mass and hear the priest and I can pray two prayers at once. My thoughts are becoming a symphony. My body sways involuntarily. And then it happens: I cannot move. It feels as though a weighted blanket has been thrown over me and the blanket has been drawn tight, like a net. I have to just sit there. Something is acting upon me.

I'm cautious about telling anyone. Had I read a similar recounting, my first assumption would be mania or psychosis. My master's degree is in special education, and I've had to recommend students for emergency psychiatric intervention when they've exhibited signs of religious mania or delusion. But I don't have the red flags: erratic mood swings, poor hygiene, bizarre habits, paranoia, or incomprehensible speech. On the contrary, I've become remarkably placid and non-reactive but not mute or disassociated. I decide to refer to Catholic books on mystical theology and I find an answer: it's called a "ligature." Just as with the root word for "religion," it means to be fused. But with mystics, it presages a very rare contemplative state characterized by a trance and the cessation of voluntary movement or speech.

The state of consciousness isn't easily described, but it's expansive and multifocal, yet obscure. The interruptive consciousness is also teaching me things. Like the time it patiently explained to me that my conception of Christ was actually Arianism (I found out what it was by googling after Mass). I learn that other things I'm being taught have names like the idea of God as the First Cause, or Augustinian theodicy. These realizations are theologically pristine and perfectly linear, yet I've never heard of them in my life. I ask myself if the thoughts are immaculate yet heretofore unknown to me, how do I know that they're my own?

   Moreover, the experiences aren't only intellectual but explicitly physical, as I have never felt ecstasy like this. Sometimes, it feels like every bit of pain I've ever felt is seeping out of the soles of my feet. At other times, it feels like a downpour of warm oil is falling upon me. My hearing and tinnitus resolved. Eventually, the arthritis will improve, and I put my canes, my wheelchairs, and my walker into storage. I'm able to use my hands to type or button my clothes. My hair has grown one foot in a year. During chemo, I developed several conditions that caused my skin and nails to turn black. I wore a medical-grade concealer. My oncologist remarks that my skin, well, it glows. Family and friends use the word, "radiant," and it's weirding them out. Me too.

   The impossible begins to happen. I know what people are praying for inside the chapel. When people get near me, I have an internal sense of urgency. It's like a guttural doorbell that rings incessantly. I'm told to tell them prayers to say. I typically can't do it. Who wants to seem like a lunatic? Things ratchet up. Friends call spontaneously, as soon as I'm done praying for them, particularly at Adoration.

   On the last Sunday after Pentecost, the "End of the World Sunday," something happens that is public and inexplicable: at Communion, I saw the priest and parishioners and the choir from above. I can only explain it to Maryanne, my Catholic twelve-step sponsor. There are aspects of it that I cannot remember. Suffice it to say, there is an invisible world of which we are unaware but that exists in tandem with the natural one. From this day forward, I operate with the firm conviction that I do not understand what is happening or what I am doing. The bible says that all men are liars. The bible also says that I am but a vapor. On the last day of Pentecost, I -- a droplet -- waded into the ocean.

Science Over Superstition

Saint John of the Cross would caution that there were definite physical effects of extraordinary religious phenomena and that these effects were not always euphoric. For instance, after his levitations (raptures), he said that he felt as though every limb was disjointed. Both he and Saint Teresa of Ávila would be bedbound for days after levitations; some saints would vomit blood after publicly-observed phenomena. These phenomena push the human organism beyond the bounds of what is accepted as possible without annihilating the organism itself. Mystics are astronauts to the realm of the Divine, rather than simply aliens exiled to earth.

Saint John of the Cross knew that Catholicism is scientific. The word, "science" comes from the Latin word, "scientia." It means to possess wisdom and to have experienced truth. Authentic science encompasses the corpus of human knowledge and the Generative Intelligence from whence it emerged. Catholicism is scientific in the way that medicine is scientific. Dogmas are spiritual laws that govern the reality that we can perceive and the unseen reality that is gradually revealed to us. Dogmas also diagnose the origins and manifestation of our separation from God. Catholicism's traditions and practices align us to reality and the truth: they affect a cure for the malady of alienation from the Divine. Catholicism is a means of reunification or fusion. In contrast, superstition relies upon an inadequate yet reflexive assessment of observed phenomena. Superstition seeks to invalidate alternative hypotheses before they are even generated. In this sense, modern man is most superstitious in his agnosticism and rationalism. Both agnosticism and rationalism are closed systems: they are hostile to possibility.

Maybe I was more arrogant than superstitious when I began my experiment in contemplative prayer without a priest as my spiritual director? I had read hagiographies and accounts of the supernatural as folktales and the peculiar reasonings of the illiterate. I was disdainful of the idea that these were manuals, rather than fairy tales. My error was vividly demonstrated to me during the Canon of the Tridentine Mass.

I remember when I was a child, visiting family in Queens, New York. We'd take the subway and I'd stand near the edge of the platform (my aunt would warn me that someone might push me onto the track, but ever the adventurer, I'd ignore her). The train would approach. Its heat would warm my face. It smelled of hot metal and electricity and the acrid air would tousle my hair. My legs and spine would vibrate as the train ground to a halt before me. More than 30 years later, the Canon feels like the approach of a train and I fear that I'm being pushed onto metaphysical tracks. I'm too medically fragile to sustain the strain: my chest heaves and one day, my legs become jello at the communion rail and an ambulance is called. The paramedics ask me questions as they lift me into the stretcher, but I'm still in the ligature and I cannot move or speak.

The paramedics wheel me past Father D. and I hear myself apologize for disrupting the Mass. I can move! From afar, he says that it doesn't matter. He tells me to remember that nothing matters, provided that Christ is in my heart. But by the time the medics wheel me into the ambulance away from Father D., I cannot move.

I can barely speak when another priest performs the last rites. I'm admitted into the ER. The nurse is surly. He requests that I perform tasks that assess my neurological function, but I'm still in the ligature and I cannot. The paramedics and nurses remind him that I didn't respond to sternum rubs (over the area where I've had a radical mastectomy). He responds that my vitals are normal and that I'm a malingerer. Tears flow past my earlobes and onto the pillow as I watch them, mute.

As the medical staff prognosticates, I consider why the ligature lifted when I heard Father D. but returned with the other priest. I remember anecdotes from the books on mystical theology: it seems that Father D. has the ability to "recall" me. With contemplatives who experience extraordinary phenomena, there is typically one priest who can break the trance. Oddly, it is not necessarily a religious superior, as in religious orders or with higher ranking clergy present. Moreover, a priest's ability to "recall" a mystic isn't evidence of demonic possession, as canonized saints were publicly recalled by priests, even as witnessed by previous popes. Whatever the inexplicable reason, Father D.'s ability is vital information, judging by the ER nurse's disgust: I'm frightened at the implications of his insinuations, but I cannot speak to defend myself. There are also accounts of contemplatives who've risen several stories in levitation, or who cannot be moved by five men if they lie on the ground. I'm terrified of the prospect of a public episode. Father D.'s baffling ability would be my solution, although he and the other priests are oblivious. I am too afraid to tell them.

What Is Love?
Love is the infinite expansion of completion. Love is perfect being. Love is the nonviolent invasion of a Healing Agent that purifies and transforms whatever It encounters while suffusing the

beloved with Itself until there is nothing left of the other. The single encounter reverberates through any subsequent encounters, transforming them into a fuller present and a limitlessly expanding future. Love apprehends reality without the fracturing and limitations induced by fear. Contemplation is union with love. Contemplation is the act of loving God and of being love. Catholicism's ultimate aim is contemplation.

Saint Teresa of Avila compared the evolution of contemplative prayer to different methods of drawing water. Before, the effects of the trance states were aggressively disruptive, like how a fire hose, if set to the highest pressure, can flay human skin. Now, my contemplative states are like tide changes. There is a predictable rhythm of altered consciousness that guides my awareness.

On Sundays, the flow is as follows: I wake up at 5:00 am and pray for an hour. I go into a trance-state and pray through two Masses; I drive home at around noon. I chat up friends over espresso. I return home to pray and then I play the Mass with Father D.'s sermon over Youtube as I nap. The last thing is not an irreverent act, and it isn't for me. It's penance for my father, a former Haitian Catholic school boarder whose face grimaces with revulsion at the mention of anything holy. He hates the Church. He hates me and my devotion. I used to hate him. By some miracle, I don't want him to die with that grimace on his face while refusing a priest, as he did when he had emergency heart surgery. A priest at the chapel had a remedy: Father D.'s French accent could be the zealous cheese for my mouse. I could play the broadcast at home within earshot of my father. The suggestion seemed ludicrous -- until I realized that my father would suddenly need to "clean the kitchen" for the duration of the broadcast, noticeably pausing during Father D.'s sermon. I'd leave Youtube on autoplay. He'd sometimes sing "Tantum Ergo," or "Salve Regina" with the videos! My nap provides cover for him to inch towards God.

One Sunday, I wake up as the broadcast ends and my father is still "cleaning". The next video is of a shrill podcaster who is overly fixated on tousling his hair. I go to change the video, but I feel an internal pause. "Beloved," something says within me, "Look at the screen." Instantaneously, I know what will happen.

The podcaster hosts a journalist from a Catholic newspaper that condemns the priestly fraternity. It's a hit piece. Their voices are strained, and the crescendo heightens with glee, positively breathless with outrage. The journalist spits out Father D.'s name like a curse. It is a byword. To them, Father D. is not a man or even human, but a black beast: a cassock-wearing priest who stands accused of sexual immorality. Father D.'s picture is frozen on the screen with an innocent smile. He cannot open his mouth.

They say that the primary accuser was a victim of previous sex abuse. I know what the journalist and the podcaster may not. I know what it is to be a girl and to tell a man, a police officer with a gun at his hip; or a counselor; or a room full of adults; or your reflection in a video camera in a recorded deposition what happened when he held you down and raped you -- but you don't even have a word it. The shame crushes you as you fumble your attempt to explain why you didn't fight or scream; or worse, why you went back or begged him not to tell, or why you added ammonia to the bathwater, that night. You stare into the camera or whisper into the phone as everything fades away and you unconsciously body-block yourself with your school bag or your trapper keeper, or your numb arms, as your chin sinks into your chest. One or more of the spectators may eventually suggest rage as the antidote to your violation: curse, and don't bless! But the wound will grow and so will the rage, little do you know. Other men will seem like him -- the boyfriend, the teacher, the priest -- but you don't know who's who anymore, and this doesn't make you a wanton woman or a liar, you want to say, but the words are caught in your throat.

Her voice is not her own. Her body is not her own. They are raping her again: her anguish is at their service. On the screen, their grins seem like snarls. Their lips glisten.

I consider the implications of priests' visibility as I zone out, staring at their mouths. Priests ascend the pulpit in traditional chapels. Their voices project above and over the faithful. The altar is roped off, as well, during Mass; however, authority does not render invincibility. Singular visibility, like the enshrouding blackness of the cassock, creates vulnerability. Christ also stood apart and elevated from the crowd. Their response was, "Tolle, tolle crucifige eum (Take him away and crucify Him)!"

Christ was True God and True Man, like us in everything but sin. Beneath the cassock or collar is a human and a man. The masculine imperative is to dominate or alter the external environment and to be affirmed for having done it. Priests affect external change and internal evolution in those surrounding them -- but they must remain above and apart. What happens when we know we'll never be truly near those surrounding us? When we never dissolve the public persona and expose the hidden wound, the thing unspeakable? What happens when we are never embraced while sobbing? What if no one ever grabs our palm and places it against their lips, and we never feel warm airflow from their mouth over our hand? I may know what it is; a priest knows what it is; an accuser may know: it is a cross. We must kiss our crosses instead and carry them. How many told Father D. what it is, in the confessional, and how many did he absolve, taking the burden off their backs?

I have a shameful epiphany. My projections and theories cannot be confirmed. If there was a room or a confessional in which the incidents occurred, only two people were in it, and their accounts would surely differ if they could both tell. The internet is a simulacrum of reality and the Bible says that all men are liars. I'm going to change the video, but it's too late. My father is standing at the entrance to the den, with a dishrag in his hand. His face is contorted with rage.

"Are they talking about Father D.?"

I nod.

"And these two are supposed to be Catholics, right?"

I nod again.

"So, they know what the sin of detraction is, against a priest? And calumny, do you know what they say about calumny, in Kreyòl? A calumny is as though you set alight a palm frond. Everyone who hears is a little fire, started by the embers that catch the wind. To atone for the calumny, you would need to catch every ember, and put out every fire. This is exactly what I've always said! All these "good Catholics" are hypocrites!" He stomps to his office and slams the door. The little girl in me whispers, Please, Papa, don't go. I was waking up to do penance for his conversion. My father would never watch another Mass or sermon again.

My throat tightens. I feel the tears -- that would really make him rage. I decided to call my sponsor, Maryanne.

Loving A Prostitute

God commanded Hosea to marry an adulteress. The marriage is a metaphor for God's love for the unfaithful children of Israel.

I've had students who've been trafficked. They seem just like other girls, to me. But whispers and stares gnaw at them and stalk them. I distract them. I tell them that they're welcome and that they've done nothing wrong, that I do not judge or condemn. They cannot look me in the eyes. I might offer candy, a kind word, or preferential seating, but I know not to get too close, and to never touch. I ask them how they're doing, and I ask how I can help. It makes them weep, or rage, or hysterical; my compassion hurts. I ask them how they can know that I won't understand…

Eventually, they get pregnant and drop out -- another pregnancy by another man soon follows, and the first baby lives with a relative. A former student will knock on my door and ask if I remember such-and-such? She's living in a hotel with a pimp and another woman. Where's the second baby? The student isn't sure. A few weeks later, in my Facebook feed, I might read a story about a high-class call girl's rotting corpse, found in a storage drum. Passers-by were alarmed by the stench and the seeping fluid. Prostitution doesn't conform to the "hooker with a heart of gold" romantic comedy cliches. Love for an adulteress is always unrequited. Before God, we are all prostitutes, even the virgins.

    I'm on the phone with Maryanne and I'm crying. It's not sobs. My tears are an oozing wound. I tell her about the video and my father. She sighs; she knows what it's like. I realize that I don't hate Father D., or the accuser, or the podcaster, or the journalist. I remember that Saint Aquinas says that to love someone means to want the good for them and that the ultimate good is God, so I love all of them. I say that I love them, and child rapists, and cannibals, and slavers, and saints, and bullies, and babies because I want God for us all, otherwise why would I care? If it were hate, I'd will their destruction even if I incurred my own in creating it. So, it's love, always love, and it aches. My heart may be the planet's biggest cathedral and I'm cramming seven billion people into a midnight Mass.

    "Let's pray, Ger," Maryanne says, "In the name of the Father, and of the Son, and of the Holy Spirit, Amen. Dear Dad, my sister Gerry and I are coming before you…" I weep in silence as Maryanne prays. Less than a year later, Maryanne dies. A friend says that grief is love persevering.

Goodnight, Father

I won't leave the Church again. Wherever Christ in the tabernacle is, there am I. I resolve that if I'm to love anyone, I will love a sinner. In this way, we bear the same burden as Christ.

One night, as I'm leaving Mass, I see Father D. with a group of men. I approach him to ask for a blessing, as a saintly priest once told me, but I stop in my tracks. I remember that women aren't allowed to get too close. Father D. sees me.

"Bonsoir mon père," I say at a distance, waving.

"À vous aussi."

I walk to my car, in silence. I pray for Father D. and the other priests each morning when I wake up. When I close my eyes, I see Father D. as a Haitian slave, although White. He's in a sugar cane field hacking through the cane with a dull machete, covered in sweat and he's bare-chested and barefoot, wearing the crude linen trousers of the field workers. Some of the cane has pierced through his chest and it's entangled his heart. He hacks and groans and sometimes he doubles over to catch his breath. He's made a little clearing in the field. Behind him are slaves of every race, urging him forward but not lifting a finger. He will have to make a way for us.

I drive away, playing the Knights Templars' "Salve Regina," on YouTube music. I see the chapel in my rearview mirror. It's not the pixelated mirage of the hit piece. The chapel is alive, with a beating heart in the tabernacle, at its center.

I Am My Ancestor's Wildest Dream

Jackson Pickney

I am my ancestor's (the Communion of Saints) wildest dreams!!! When I think of being Black and Catholic, I cannot help but think of it as asking a fish what it is like being a fish; do they know that their water is wet. It is all I know today. I have been Black all my life. I have been Christian, thanks be to God, for as long as I can remember.

Ever since Theology-101 class, in 1994, had given me a clearer look at history I had doubts about Protestantism's approach to Christianity. I converted to the Catholic Church in 2008 in my head and heart, and I came into the Church on the Easter Vigil of 2010. It is such a blessing to know the continuation and completion of first century Judaism, the fullness of Christianity, the Ony Holy

Catholic Apostolic faith. Knowing this truth truly sets you free.

Who would think that according to some people today, I am required to self-identify as Black too, whatever that means? Trust me folks my skin color doesn't wash off at night and no one gets to define what it is to be Black. I define it every day by the very life I live. I am Black and I will not be defined by someone's prejudice, stereotype, or derogatory narrative. Black excellence is the goal, a credit to my family name. I am adopted and my adoptive grandfather told me when I was a little boy, "You're a Pickney now and that means something." Thank you, grandpa, I will live up to this name!

On Being Black

"Say it loud, I'm Black and I'm proud!" - James Brown

Never has a people who started so far behind come so far. From slavery to the presidency of the country. We have arrived and we are not oppressed, except for between our two ears. Control the mind and you control the man. Do not believe the hype, America is a great country, and it is the best place on the planet for Blacks. There are Black immigrants still migrating to the United States for a reason. You can 'make it' here.

We are a proud people with a beautiful past of overcoming major obstacles. Slavery, Slave codes, Jim Crow Laws, Ku Klux Klan lynch mobs, segregation, prejudice, and outright lies about just being born with a certain amount of melanin means the lesser desirable life.

We are victors, not victims, and should not ever buy into the modern lie of because of skin color you are better or worse off because of the amount or lack thereof of melanin in said skin. Your attitude and aptitude will determine a lot of how your story in America will be written. The content of your character and the very choices you make the difference. Choose the good! Larry Elder says it best. Complete your education. Get a job. Get married and have your children with your husband/wife only. Do this, in this order and you will be successful in America.

For as far as I can remember, the goal of being Black was to prove that we are just as good as if not better than our Caucasian counterparts. Worthy of our seat at the American table.

I think the of the military examples of the 54th Massachusetts Volunteer Infantry Regiment first Black unit in the union army during the civil war, 369th Infantry Regiment also known as the Harlem Hellfighters World War I Black unit, the 332nd Fighter Group the Tuskegee airmen who never lost a bomber, they escorted, to enemy action during World War II, Montford Point Marines first Black Marine Corp. Unit, 555th Parachute Infantry Battalion first Black airborne unit, the Carl Brashear story as portrayed by Cuba Gooding Jr., in the movie 'Men of Honor'.

All of these dispel the myth that we as Blacks were less than capable of success in military service. With military service, education, entertainment, business, politics, and the sports arenas we have proven ourselves worthy of a seat at the table of America. Have a seat! Our history is American history. Assimilate and be blessed.

Economic Success vs. Political power
"Let down your bucket where you are!" – Booker T. Washington

The and/both Catholic concept is best applied here. We should seek both, political and economic success, as a people, but one may pay off better than the other. We have reached the highest heights of political success in America, president of the United States, where has that gotten us?

From the perspective of my 46 years, nowhere and I venture to say race relations are worse for it today as I write this. Economic success as a people on the other hand may be the best thing for us.

"The individual who can do something that the world wants done will, in the end, make his way regardless of his race." – Booker T. Washington

Irrespective of who is in political office, friend or foe of my people, economic success makes most people empowered enough to withstand and rise above bad political policies. Trust me when I say this, Warren Buffet does not care who is in the White House, and best believe, he is not affected by it. His wealth insulates him to it.

Matter of fact, most politicians are coming to him with their hands out looking for a donation. When you are poor, bad political policies are the boot on your neck. It hamstrings a people. The

Nany state, big government, is the socialism of our day here in America. Yes, the welfare state was started with good intentions, but the safety net of society has incentivized the worst of humanity, the sin of sloth. This also has led to the breakdown of the family. When the government is daddy, the true father of the home is let off the hook from his responsibilities, such as, marrying the mother of his children, being a provider, and protector of his family.

There is no better wake-up call than becoming a father. It is time to kill the boy and become a man, but in many cases now due to government programs, he is kicked out of the house and, thereby, enabled to continue this bad behavior to go and do it again to other women. Many of the ills of low-income Black and White families is due to government intervention thru these well-intended handouts. Give a man a wheelchair and he will forget how to walk. I want my people, all Americans, to run again!

Top of the economic food chain in America today are Asian people. They lead in all economic categories college admittance and graduation, household income, successful marriage rates, homeownership, etc. Can you name one prominent Asian politician? We as a people would learn well from their example. Strong families, low to no divorce rates, and an extreme emphasis on education. True education frees you.

Civil War in the Community; Blacks vs. Niggas
"You know who the most racist people are? Black people. I hate niggas too." - Chris Rock

The problem with my people is cultural. I would venture to say we do not even have a culture.

Most bourgeoisie middle-class Black people want a fair shake, and when we do not get it, we scream racism, but is it? No one wants to be seen as some stereotype. The actual leaders that would give a good example and lead our people out of the victim mentally are ignored.

You really must ask yourself, why people like Robert "Bob" Woodson, Walter Williams, Thomas Sowell, Shelby Steele, Glenn Loury, Coleman Hughes, Jason Riley, and Clarence Thomas are not in the National Museum of African American History and Culture, and never will be. The Black conservative voice is greatly demonized and sidelined to the detriment of the people. Cannot have these Blacks thinking and doing for themselves.

Democratic party storytime narratives and Marxist race theories have little to no influence on the Black conservative mindset. The Democrats may lose their most solid vote base. Cannot have that! Black conservative thought runs counter to the oppressed victimhood narrative.

We preach self-reliance and a to-do for self-mentality. For this, the Black conservative is labeled an enemy to the people by those profiting off the mind shackling of my people. All our skin folks ain't kinfolk. The race hustlers' social activists Sambos, the real enemy to the people, who earn a check from keeping past wrongs, current slights, and any grievance going keep the emotionally unstable in the community in a constant enflamed volatile state.

Victimhood is attractive. My failures are not my fault; it's the man keeping me down. This just is not true. You do have self-determination. You do have self-agency! As dem boys from Atlanta, Outcast ft Goodie Mob, once said, *"You need to git up git out and git something...How will you make it if you never even try...Cuz you and I, got to do for you and I."*

The so-called social activists are not about creating solutions because that would put them out of business, and their business is very good right now. The misinformed lower rings of our community are preyed upon by these sellouts and are woefully misled by those who benefit from their ignorance to keep us in our place, waiting on Massa government to make things right.

If White people are so oppressive, why are we depending on them for our faculties? We must do it for ourselves! We have, and we can again. Billy Bob and the boys in the pickup truck with the rebel flags are not the problems! The social activist and the mainstream media constantly telling me and mine we are oppressed are the problem. This brainwashing must end.

> *"The lesson taught at this point by human experience is simply this, that the man who will get up will be helped up; and the man who will not get up will be allowed to stay down. Personal independence is a virtue and it is the soul out of which comes the sturdiest manhood. But these can be no independence without a large share of self-dependence, and this virtue cannot be bestowed. It must be developed from within."* – Fredrick Douglass

Systematic racism is a myth. Do you know why? All the previously mentioned Black men and women have already overcome, risen above, and succeeded in America. It is a myth because of my testimony. I attest to this. I have privilege. I was raised in a two-parent Christian home, which is the biggest head above shoulders starter kit for success in America. Educational success was encouraged. Having parents that give a rip about you and bust their ass to make it happen for you. I am not the smartest, fastest, strongest, but I beat the supposed 'systemic' racism system. Even if there is such a thing as 'systemic' racism system, the evidence itself bares witness that it is not so powerful that you can overcome it.

In my past, I have been told, by those who cannot see past perception, that XYZ individual is racist. Well, XYZ hired me for a job I was completely not qualified for but willing to learn. Well, you're different. Well, then, we should all be "different".

"A credit to my race", Hattie McDaniel's acceptance speech for Academy Award for Best Supporting Actress, *Gone with the Wind* (1939). Hattie is right. Be a credit to your race.

On Being Catholic

Here is the scary part, it's all true! – Timothy Gordon ('Why Lourdes Proves the Catholic Church True')

"From animal to men, from heathen to Christian."
– GK Chesterton,

The biggest question of life is, does God exist? I got to admit for me, Pascal's Wager, really boils this down to its rawest essences:
- If God REALLY exists, and we believe (= bet that God exists), we have an infinite gain (heaven).
- If God REALLY exists, and we don't believe that, then we have the potential of an infinite loss (hell, or at least eternal separation from God).
- If God really does NOT EXIST, and we believe that God exists, we essentially lose nothing.
- If God really does NOT EXIST, and we believe that God doesn't exist, we essentially gain nothing.

Eternity is a long time to find out you were wrong on the most essentials.

Now that we got that out of the way, God does indeed exist, but which God? All other world religions are man trying to ascend to God. Judaism, our elder brothers before us, and Christianity are God coming down to man and showing us the way. In particular, in Christianity, it is the eternal Logos himself, in the flesh, to which he said, "*I am the way, and the truth and life. No man cometh to father but by me.*" Yeah, I know not much wiggle room there.

Okay, Christianity yes, but why Catholic? Being Catholic is the best way to live a happy life. Not in the way of the world, happy, but in the way of our Creator. There is a God, and we will worship Him. Jesus Christ, the eternal Logos, the Jewish messiah, Himself established the Catholic Church. If you are truly looking for Him and his way, you have found it if you are Roman Catholic.

History is on our side! *"Roman Catholicism, Christian church that has been the decisive spiritual force in the history of Western civilization... The Roman Catholic Church traces its history to Jesus Christ and the Apostles. Over the course of centuries, it developed a highly sophisticated theology and an elaborate organizational structure headed by the papacy, the oldest continuing absolute monarchy in the world."* – (Roman Catholicism - Britannica.com)

The supernatural proves it, just ask anyone who had been delivered from demonic possession through the Church's ministry of exorcism. Other examples down through the years are the bodies of multiple incorruptible saints that smelling like flowers, the image of Our Lady of Guadalupe, the Shroud of Turin, the annual liquefaction of the blood of Saint Januarius, multiple miraculous (seventy 70 verified) healings at Lourdes, France since 1858, Multiple secular witnesses to the miracle of the sun at Fatima Portugal 1917 and the scientific evidence proves of the Holy Eucharist miracles where the Eucharist, the consecrated communion host, which by faith holy mother church teaches is the body blood soul and divinity of Christ, turns into heart tissue (who needs faith when it turns into what it is, what a glorious miracle).

The One, Holy Catholic and Apostolic Church is everything that sacred scripture and holy Tradition say the kingdom of God here on earth is: *"He said therefore: To what is the kingdom of God like, and whereunto shall I resemble it? It is like to a grain of mustard seed, which a man took and cast into his garden, and it grew and became a great tree, and the birds of the air lodged in the branches thereof. And again, he said: Whereunto shall I esteem the kingdom of God to be like? It is like to leaven, which a woman took and hid in three measures of meal, till the whole was leavened."* – Luke 13: 18-20

> *"The kingdom of heaven is like unto a treasure hidden in a field. Which a man having found, hid it, and for joy thereof goeth, and selleth all that he hath, and buyeth that field. Again the kingdom of heaven is like to a merchant seeking good pearls. Who when he had found one pearl of great price, went his way, and sold all that he had, and bought it. Again the kingdom of heaven is like to a net cast into the sea, and gathering together of all kind of fishes. Which, when it was filled, they drew out, and sitting by the shore, they chose out the good into vessels, but the bad they cast forth. So shall it be at the end of the world. The angels shall go out, and shall separate the wicked from among the just. And shall cast them into the furnace of fire: there shall be weeping and gnashing of teeth."* - Matthew (13: 44-50)

"Another parable he spoke to them: The kingdom of heaven is like to leaven, which a woman took and hid in three measures of meal, until the whole was leavened." – Matthew (13-33)

We are not perfect, but we strive for perfection according to Christ's command. Look to the saints in Heaven, the Church triumphant, for this example of perfection and do like wish. Everyone here on Earth, the Church militant, is still running the race.

Some are running faster than others, some not running at all and actively hampering others.

> *"The church is a field hospital"* – Pope Francis.

Being Black and Catholic in America
> *"I'm concerned about the decline of values. You don't see a lot of honesty."* – Thomas Sowell

The American experiment was based on the founding of a nation on ideals and documents the declaration of independence, constitution, and the bill of rights, not a race. America is not founded on a collective ethnicity! We are the melting pot of the world. Major problems arise with the Marxism race theories of yesterday and today pitting one race over against one another. We are all Americans, from the born here native to America to the newest naturalized India Indian immigrant citizen.

America is still a protestant nation and Blacks are in the minority. So, we are a minority within a minority. You may be the only Black face in the pew. What else is new? Go to any major Fortune 500 company and you'll see similar numbers of us. The few and the proud.

> *"A racist country does elect a Black man twice."*
> – Ben Shapiro

> *"What should we do about racism in America?"*
> – Mike Wallace, *"Stop talking about it!"*
> – Morgan Freeman (60 Minutes interview, 2005)

I find it very interesting that most Black Catholics are more concerned with being Black, again whatever that is than being Catholic. I think of myself as Catholic first and hopefully a faithful one. Whatever else I am in this life, a man, friend, husband, father, veteran, employee, and Black, I believe benefits, is enlightened by and is uplifted by me being a member of the body of Christ, the Church militant, salt and light here and now on earth, looking forward to graduation to the Church triumphant into the beatific vision. Christ is enough.

"Black Supremacy is as dangerous as White supremacy, and God is not interested merely in the freedom of Black men, God is interested in the freedom of the whole human race and in the creation of a society where all men can live together as brothers." – Dr. Martin Luther King Jr speech at DePauw University, 1960.

My Skin Color Wasn't Enough For My Salvation

David L. Gray

All my life I tried to be 'Black' until, one day, I realized that I just had to be Catholic. It was a very long journey to that realization, but it was the most important accidental destination that I had ever arrived at. Allow me to tell you a little about it.

The 30-Year Mission of Hiding Oreo Cookies
By the time I was in the fourth grade for the first time, I think my stepfather Roy had reached the firm conclusion that I was not culturally 'Black', and he made it his mission to correct that defect in my character.

If I must admit it, Roy was right. I did want to be White like my friends. I wanted blond hair that I could blow away from my

face when it got into my eyes like Mark and Jeremy always did. I wanted freckles on my face like Robert. Except for Sonya Byars and Delores Jones, all the girls I liked were White. I was quite the ugly little boy back then, so I am not surprised that any of the girls who I liked girl ever liked me back, and I also realized that I was different from my friends when my pursuit of Beth Ann abruptly ended when she said to me, "Why don't you try to get a girlfriend who looks like you?"

On the first day of Roy's mission to turn me culturally Black, my bedroom was filled with images that you expect to find in the bedroom of any ten-year-old White boy in 1982. The first thing he did was tear down a floor rug of the Fonzie from 'Happy Days' that I had hanging on my wall.

"Are you Black or are you White?"

"Black?" I responded inquisitively, perhaps guessing.

"Then why do you have this picture of a White man on your wall?"

Shrugging, "I don't know," pausing, grasping, "I like him?"

"Who looks more like an animal; them or us?"

What an odd question I remember thinking. I had never thought about it, but I suppose Black people do look like monkeys, I mused to myself.

"We do?"

"No! Look at them," as he was holding the Fonzie carpet in his hand. "Look at their stringy hair. They look like animals, and smell like dogs when they get wet!"

That was an odd thing Dad just said, I thought to myself, I had been swimming every summer with my friends and had even been around Jeremy and Mark when they got out of the shower during sleepovers. I only remember them smelling like chlorine and soap when I was around them.

"You are not one of them! And give me those KISS albums too. You don't listen to that music!"

Roy took my whole KISS album collection and I never saw them again. More of Roy's project to remove the 'White' from me included putting me on a youth football team on the predominately Black Westside of Warren, Ohio, taking me on outings to the projects, also on that side of town, to footrace in the streets against his friend's sons, who I always beat, and drawing me into frequent discussions about how Blacks are superior to Whites in sports.

It was taken as a personal affront to Roy if one of my White friends ever bested me at anything athletic. He would not harbor it, but his anger about my losses began to turn me into being ruthless. Heretofore, I used to make it point to lose to my friends on purpose, just because I believed that it was nice to let your friends win every once in and while, but Roy was now making me choose between the kids in the neighborhood liking to play with me or earning his approval.

It turned out that spent the next thirty years of my life trying to be who Roy thought I should be. The belief that my skin color was the most important thing about me, and that I had something essential in common with other people who had my same skin color, was the dogma that guided everything about my life for the next three decades. From switching high schools to one that was predominantly Black to beating up random White boys in High school, to graduating from a Historical Black University, to becoming a Prince Hall Freemasonry (a predominately Black sect of Freemasonry), to joining Omega Psi Phi Fraternity (the Blackest Greek-letter fraternity), to never dating outside my race, to rejecting Christianity (the White man's religion), to always voting Democrat (the party that helps Black folk), to how I dressed, the music I listened to, the TV shows I watched, to a litany of other things, I tried as hard as I could to appear to be Black, and I was scared to death of anyone finding out that I was just posing.

Death, Life, and I Never Heard of Black Catholic
Being an Agnostic eventually catches up with you. Making your own private moral laws is a tremendously foolish errand, and it is one that found me ready to end it all. Killing myself was a much better option than living with the dire consequences of my choices. I loved my wife and my three daughters, but going to prison for nine years for embezzling a few hundred thousand dollars sounded

like a brand of suffering that I could not handle. Heretofore, the worst thing that had ever happened to me in my privileged life was having my luggage still sitting in Australia after my body had landed in New Zealand. No, I would not suffer this life and I would not allow my wife, at that time, and my daughters to suffer with me.

So, I put a plastic bag around my head, tightened a bedsheet around my neck, tied it to the headboard, and started turning around in the bed to tighten it up, so that I could suffocate myself and die. As I was on about the second and half-turn, I heard a voice.

"I love you. I am here"

I stopped. I took the plastic bag off my head. My eyes got big. Who said that? I looked around and everyone was sleeping in the jail cell, but I knew the voice I had just heard was immediately in my ear, despite the bag being around my head.

Who said that? At that moment, somehow through divine inspiration, I awoke to the realization that it was Jesus Christ, which was the most ridiculous answer my head could have ever come up with, and that is why I immediately knew it was true. In other words, the answer that came from within me was so far off the mark of any coherent thought that I would have ever conjured up on my own, that I knew that I did not come up with it. It did not come from my own intellectual capacity. Fictional characters from the White man's religion do not speak to people.

I began to follow Jesus that day. I read the first three Gospels (*Matthew, Mark,* and *Luke*) that night and I believed. I suppose I was a mere Protestant Christian at that point, but eventually, that whole protesting thing did not make any sense to me. It seemed completely stupid and inconsistent with the sacred Scriptures to have so many competing denominations; all of them proclaiming the same Bible, claiming to have the same Holy Spirit; yet, all of them proudly arrive at competing conclusions with each other. Protestantism seemed like a bad movie or a joke without a punchline. I didn't know which.

I could not imagine a world in which God left His people in confusion. What type of God goes through the effort of providing a whole path of salvation to redeem us; inspires His prophets with testimony about the coming Messiah, sends His angel Gabriel to announce the Incarnation to Mary, conceives in her His only begotten and beloved Son; gives His Son a ministry to proclaim the good news, gathers disciples, heals the sick, feeds the hungry, cast out demons, sacrifice His life, and then comes back from the dead to spend another forty days with His apostles who then establishes a Church, to then allows His people to just make up stuff as they go along and be utterly confused and competing with each other about what is true? If Protestantism is true, then either God is sadistic and cruel or there is no God.

I could not settle for either of those conclusions, so in 2006, while I was still in prison, I set out to discover what happened to the Churches in the Bible, and when I discovered that, historically, the Catholic Church today could prove that they are the same community of Churches established by Christ Jesus through His apostles, I almost had a mental breakdown.

First off, I had never heard of a Black Catholic before. I had no idea that Black people could even become Catholic, and I had no idea what the Catholic religion was. It looked weird, over the top, and very White. I just could not be a Black Catholic. It was enough that my political views were already changing. I was not going to go and join the Whitest religion next to Mormonism. What was next? Tuck my sweaters into my pants? Wear a North face jacket? Marry someone outside of my race and fit perfectly into that 'sellout' stereotype? Not me! They ain't gonna call me an Uncle Tom!

I should have never read that *Catechism of the Catholic Church*. Now, I no longer believed that abortion is a woman's right. What? I'm Republican now? Barack Obama is bad? This is crazy! On top of that, having been awoken to the truth, I felt as if had no choice but to become a Catholic. Not only was the historical case solid, that today's Catholic Church is the very same Church of the Apostles, but everything they believe is substantiated and affirmed by tradition and Scripture. Despite me being quite hesitant of taking this next step, I did not understand how I could not be obedient to the truth; nor how I could reject the gift that Christ Jesus left us in His Church and the Sacraments He gave Her for our sanctification on the journey home.

I had no idea that following Jesus would lead me to the Catholic Church, but there I was on August 8, 2006, on the Feast of Saint Dominic De Guzman, being confirmed by Father Patrick Toner into the One, Holy, Catholic, and Apostolic Church; taking Saint Joseph as my confirmation name.

She is Most Beautiful and Worthy of Protection

I loved the liturgy of the Catholic Mass from the very first day of worship. The ritual, the order, the form, the silence, the reverence. The liturgy was like a beautiful woman that day – the most beautiful woman in the world. She was perfect and elegant in all her ways; all men could do was adore her; she was silent, but when she spoke everyone gave her their full attention. We all bought her gifts, but in her generosity and kindness, her gift to us was far greater than that which she received from us. She dismissed us, but we could not get enough of her, so we returned, again, again, and again.

It is a shame that people dismiss her beauty and want to change her. She is enough on her own and does not need our help. For, the presence of God is with her, and only comes to be present to us, in her, and through her. She is enough just how she is, and she does not even care what I look like or what I have. She only desires the best for me and is always there for me. She is perfect just how she is.

Yet, what a wonderful occasion it was for me to discover her many forms. She is a lady with the most beautiful outer garments but never changing in her essence. The first day I beheld her in her garments from the East is a day that I will never forget. The divine liturgy of Saint Gregory the Great (The Divine Liturgy) captured me like nothing else ever has. This was true worship. It was a mystery and mystical all at once. For the second time, I felt as if I had come home to the Catholic Church.

Just as it was with my first Novus Ordo Mass, I did not know what to expect that day I decided to worship at Saint Peter & Paul Byzantine Catholic Church in Warren, Ohio. I had never witnessed a Catholic Mass; I had never been to a Catholic wedding, funeral, or even watched one on television, nor did I have any foreknowledge of what to expect the first time I worshipped in the Divine Liturgy of Saint John Chrysostom.

My reasoning for venturing out from my parish back then was because I knew something was 'off' there. I had only been a Catholic for six years, and four of those years were in prison, where we were blessed to have the same priest, Father Patrick Toner, who offered the same liturgy, with no deviations from the General Instruction of the Roman Missal. The first time I had even heard music at Mass was when I was released from prison and started riding my bike to daily Mass at Saint Brigid in Xenia, Ohio, and I didn't like the music at all. All those years of having silence before and during the liturgy spoiled me.

In 2012, I was still extremely happy and joyful to be a Catholic, but Saint James Catholic Church felt dead to me, and diabolical things were going on there. And it made me sad because that was the Church that was situated right across from the grandmother's house, which she bequeathed to me and where I was now living. I had been to a few other parishes in Warren, Ohio; all of which seemed to be spiritually healthier than Saint James, but I did not get that sense of feeling 'at home' as I did the first instance I walked into that 12x16 foot room in prison.

All that changed that day I found the Byzantine liturgy. I do not even know if I knew what the word 'Byzantine' meant, but I did gather from the website of Peter & Paul that they were in communion with Rome. What is peculiar is that of all the times I have visited Peter & Paul since nothing was like that first time.

It all seemed otherworldly; it was mysterious and full of mystique; full of odors without a hint of being arduous. It was just simply transcendental. I could not believe this thing was happening in my small town. What was this? What is behind that veil? The doors open – the doors shut. Why are they kissing those icons? What are they singing? Is that Greek? They are singing the whole Mass? Who does that? Why is the Creed slightly different? Those are not the readings for this Sunday! Are they really going to spoon-feed me the Body and Blood of Jesus Christ? I did not know the history of this liturgy, but I had a sure sense that this was as close as I was ever going to get to true worship.

I had fallen in love again, but around the same time, Ellen and Melinda who I had met online had suggested that I visit Saint Dominic's Catholic Church in Youngstown. It was a mission parish of the Order of Preachers in an area of the city that was once one of the most dangerous neighborhoods in the entire country. Father Maturi, the pastor of Saint Dominic's, had become nationally known for having cleaned up the neighborhood after one of his parishioners was shot and killed after leaving Mass.

My belief in mystery, order, and form being able to be found in the Novus Ordo had been restored by Saint Dominic's. In fact, it was the first time that I had ever encountered the communion rail with kneelers and the absence of lay ministers of the Holy Eucharist. I felt like I was back in prison, except for the beautiful gothic structure, art, confessional booths, and statues. My heart was tugging at me to return to the East, but I had made friends with Father Maturi and he began supporting the work I was doing to promote the cause of canonization for Father Augustus Tolton, so I joined Saint Dominic's, but once a month I would return East, either to Saint Peter & Paul or the Basilica & National Shrine of Our Lady of Lebanon, which is a Maronite Catholic Church in North Jackson, Ohio.

Once I moved to Columbus, Ohio I thought again about changing rites. I would often worship at Holy Resurrection, which is a Melkite Rite Eastern Catholic Church. One of my fondest memories there was when Father Ignatius Harrington allowed me to observe him perform the 'Liturgy of Preparation,' in which the Priest and Deacon offer a very ritualistic and meaningful preparation and blessing of the bread and wine that will become the Body and Blood of our Lord Jesus Christ.

It could have happened. I think was ready to change rites for good, but I was a bit put off by the fact that whenever the liturgy had ended and everyone gathered in the adjacent room for refreshments, they were all speaking in their own language and showed absolutely no interest in me being there. I kept trying to affirm to myself that that is not what matters the most; that I was there for worship, not to make friends, but who was I to ignore the fact that I was created to be not only in communion with God but with others?

I grew up around Greek, Yugoslavian, and Lebanese people, and figured it was more of that same-ole weariness and suspicious of Blacks that was present here in Columbus, but if I had not moved to Saint Louis, Missouri, I might have committed to trying to welcome myself among them, rather than waiting for them to welcome me. Heck, my first elementary school crush was on a Lebanese girl, and I love Greek chicken. These were my people too!

I always wonder if I had found the Traditional Latin Mass first. Not long after I had worshipped at Peter & Paul, I had found Queen of the Holy Rosary Parish in Vienna, Ohio. It was standing room only for this woman, and her Roman beauty and rarity far exceeded my imagination. If not for the fact that I had already met her older sister, I might have fallen for her, but if I could not have her sister then I would not settle for anything close to her.

The door is still open to moving permanently to the East. Here in Saint Louis, I have made it a habit to worship in the Byzantine Rite whenever I am available, but, for now, I am happy just to visit with her as a reminder of what home feels like. To have such a place we can call 'home' during our pilgrimage here on Earth is important.

One Mission Fails and Another Begins
It did happen suddenly for me, as over the years I met more and more culturally Black Catholics. I would visit their liturgies, and I found them to be a people who kept wanting to change her garments into something worldly, Protestant, and altogether ugly. I become angry over time at the sight of them wanting to change everything about her but did not want to change how they voted in federal elections or change their pseudo-religion, and, thereby, fundamentally incapable of transforming the world itself into a type of liturgy. The culturally Black Catholics I met struck me as being idolaters – putting every before God - and I did not want to be anything like them.

I find it a bit sad that my breaking point came when I was worshipping at a predominately Black Catholic Church in Columbus,

Ohio and I saw myself posing as someone who I wasn't. This was not the liturgy I loved; in fact, this liturgy here was even far beneath the sacredness and reverence of the liturgy I fell in love with it in prison. Yet, there I was clapping, signifying, disturbing, and warring with the liturgy by walking around exchanging happy greetings as if it were a sign of peace. I was just trying to be Black, but I had to make a choice that day. I was either going to keep posing as a cultural Black and keep doing culturally Black stuff or I was going to be a Catholic. I did not see a path through which I could be both. If being an idolater and a race essentialist is what it meant to be a Black Catholic, then it was far beneath the life she was calling me to, and far beneath the divine culture into which my soul yearned.

From that day forward, I decided that whatever remained of the last vestiges of being culturally Black; of whatever I was still clinging onto, I let them go, I forgave Roy, and I abandoned his project for good. I decided to be Catholic alone – it was enough – it was sufficient for my salvation - and any label people wanted to give me would be formed and governed, not by my race, but by my faith.

I decided that if they called me a Black man, they would know that I am Catholic first and that my faith informs who I am culturally. I decided that if they wanted to call me a conservative, then they would know that I am Catholic first and that my faith informs every one of my actions and inactions. I rejected the humanist and naturalist idea that being fully Catholic meant I was being my full Black self. For, whatever that meant, it was tremendously far beneath becoming my full supernatural self in Christ Jesus. Whatever they wanted to call me; husband, father, theologian, etcetera, they would know that the fact that I am a Catholic first, shapes everything else about me.

I figured that if I let them know that, then they would know that my life has an end destination that is not of this world. Truly, the divisive race constructs have everything in common with Hell and certainly nothing in common with my end destination, which is Heaven.

I finally accepted the fact that I do not have to be like everyone else, and I do not have to be the person who other people think I should be. I could just be who God is forming me to be through His grace and through the liturgy, and that is me, who is like Him. That is who I will be and how I will be!

NOVENA TO FATHER AUGUSTUS TOLTON
For the Spiritual Welfare of the Black American Community
Read more at: http://www.toltonnovena.org/novena/

FIRST PRAYER
FOR THE SPIRITUAL ANCHORING
OF THE BLACK COMMUNITY

O' Father Augustus Tolton, whose faith was grounded in Christ Jesus at an early age, pray the same for all of the Black community in America, so that together they might be unified in one faith, one Lord, one Baptism, and God. Pray Father Tolton for the Black community to find and to love that same fullness of their faith that you found through the Catholic Church, and that the Church would find a deeper fullness of itself in that community. Pray Father Tolton for the Holy Eucharist to become the source and summit of Christian life in the Black community and for that unique Presence of Christ Jesus to work to conform all peoples into His image before God the Father. Amen.

SECOND PRAYER
FOR THE MORAL FORMATION
OF THE BLACK COMMUNITY

Pray O' Father Augustus Tolton, teacher of truth, for the moral formation of the youth in the Black community in America. Pray for their moral grounding in the teachings of Christ our Lord, so that they might be living witnesses of the Beatitudes. Pray Father Tolton for a strengthening and fortification of the Holy Spirit in the Black community so that it might be guided and protected in all Truth, and thereby able to withstand all assaults by the Evil One. Amen.

The Novena to Fr. Augustus Tolton
for the Spiritual Welfare of the Black American Community

THIRD PRAYER
FOR THE STABILITY AND STRENGTH OF MARRIAGES AND FAMILIES IN THE BLACK COMMUNITY

Strong families and marriages are the woven threads that have always proved to be most beneficial for all healthy societies. Pray O' Father Augustus Tolton that all husbands will love their wives as Christ loved the Church and love their wives as their own bodies. Pray that each wife will embrace her role as a type of Church in the household and embrace her husband and children as members of her body. Pray Father Tolton for the sanctity and dignity of marriages in the Black community in America and to the end of the sexual impurity and promiscuity that has led to far too many fatherless homes. Pray for the restoration of true Christ-like masculinity for Black men, and for women to look upon our Blessed Mother as a beckon of faithfulness and womanhood. Amen.

FOURTH PRAYER
FOR PEACE IN THE BLACK COMMUNITY

O' Father Augustus Tolton, servant of Peace, pray for an end of all forms of violence and for an everlasting peace in the Black community in America. Dear servant of the King of Peace, violence against each other betrays our progress and robs us of our future. Pray then Father Tolton that we all might know Christ Jesus enough so that we will see Him in each other. Pray then O' Father Tolton that in the pursuit of peace we might go from seeing Jesus in each other, to loving each other through Him, and cooperating with all that grace empowers us to bring the indwelling of Christ more fully out of each other. Pray Father Tolton for the reign of Peace throughout the world, and even more especially in communities that are harmed by persistent violence. Amen.

FIFTH PRAYER
FOR GOOD EDUCATIONAL OPPORTUNITIES IN THE BLACK COMMUNITY

The doors of opportunity in the world are open to all, and are open even more fully to those who have been educated. Pray O' Father Augustus Tolton, teacher of children, for the Holy Spirit's gifts of wisdom, understanding, and knowledge to pour out abundantly over the Black community in America, and that the schools and universities that service these communities will be blessed with the resources, staff, and faculty they need to achieve their goals. Pray for Catholic schools and universities' fidelity to the teachings of the Church, and that they might open their doors to all, especially to the poor and to the disadvantaged. Amen.

SIXTH PRAYER
FOR GAINFUL ECONOMIC OPPORTUNITIES IN THE BLACK COMMUNITY

O' Father Augustus Tolton, as we seek your intercession for the spiritual needs of the Black community in America, we also come to you dear servant of God to ask for your prayers for their material needs. Pray Father Tolton for those in the Black community to have good economic opportunities in their community to find gainful employment or to start a business, so that all might have the resources they need to provide for themselves, their family, and their Church. Pray Father Tolton that God might fill in all of us the spirit of a cheerful giver so that we might remember that all that has been given to us we will, in return, give back. Amen.

SEVENTH PRAYER
FOR THE END OF ABORTION
IN THE BLACK COMMUNITY

Far too much treasure of the Black community in America has been lost through the tragedy of abortion. Pray O' Father Augustus Tolton, for a quickening of the Holy Spirit in the Black community so that its conscience will be awakened to know that each child conceived belongs to God, and that God has given each child a plan and purpose for its life. Pray for an end of sexual objectification, adultery, and pre-marital sex that paves the way to compounded bad decisions. Pray that medical professionals will learn to see and recognize the beauty of all pre-natal children, even those that may be born different than us. Pray Father Tolton for all women and men who have in some way participated in abortions for their forgiveness and healing. Pray for all pregnant women to have all of the help and support that they need to bring their child safely into the world, so that it might have the opportunity to know, love, and serve God in this life and the next. Amen.

EIGHTH PRAYER
FOR MORE CATHOLIC EVANGELISTS
TO THE BLACK COMMUNITY

O' Father Augustus Tolton, who always sought out new opportunities to reach out to the community, pray O' faithful servant of God for the Lord to send more faithful evangelists of the Gospel into the Black communities in America. Pray Father Tolton that the Lord might send us more like you to point God's children to the light and love of Christ Jesus through the lenses of the Catholic Church. And pray Father Tolton that wherever the faithful evangelist might go that he or she will have the courage to speak only what God has given them to say, and that their words will fall upon fertile soil. Amen.

NINTH PRAYER
FOR MORE VOCATIONS TO THE PRIESTHOOD DIACONATE, AND CONSECRATED LIFE FROM THE BLACK COMMUNITY

O' Father Augustus Tolton intercede for us and pray that as the Eternal Father sent you that He will send more from the Black community in America to serve God's people as Priests, Deacons, and consecrated Religious. Pray Father Tolton for the Church's cup to overflow with blessings from vocations of men and women responding to their call to serve God's children in love. Amen.

If You Enjoyed This Book, Check Out These Others at Saint Dominic's Media
http://www.saintdominicsmedia.com

Since its publishing in 2018, *The Divine Symphony: An Exordium to the Theology of the Catholic Mass*, by David L. Gray has been consistently called the best book ever written about the liturgy of the Church.

This book consists of four very accessible and easy-to-read movements that narrate, explore, and explains the meaning, mystery, theology, history, symbolism, and continuity of the Catholic Mass.

The Liturgy of Gregory the Theologian: Critical Text with Translation and Commentary, by Dr. Nichols Newman, offers a new edition, translation, and commentary of the Greek Liturgy of St. Gregory the Theologian. In this discussion of the Greek text, which exists alongside a Coptic version, the origins of the liturgy and its programmatic use in the turbulent theological world of the fourth century are discovered. offers a new translation of several of Remigius dei Girolami's political works, the *De Bono Communi, De Bono Pacis, Sermones de Pace,* and the *De Iustitia* is offered.

www.ingramcontent.com/pod-product-compliance
Lightning Source LLC
Chambersburg PA
CBHW050323010526
44119CB00003B/78